TRIUMPH HOUSE
Poetry with a Purpose

THE ULTIMATE COLLECTION OF RHYMING VERSE 2000

Edited by

Steve Twelvetree

First published in Great Britain in 2000 by
TRIUMPH HOUSE
Remus House,
Coltsfoot Drive,
Peterborough, PE2 9JX
Telephone (01733) 898102

HB ISBN 1 86161 812 3
SB ISBN 1 86161 817 4

FOREWORD

Since the first blossoming movement of contemporary verse many people have turned their back on the purest form; of poems that rhyme, and scan easily on the untrained eye. Not only has this forced many of the traditionalists to take a back bench in their pursuit of poetic fame but many of its would-be followers have been driven away by the complexity of the modern style.

We asked our poets to challenge the modern movement and help us to compile an ultimate collections of traditional rhyming verse. So why not read on to share the true enjoyment of poetry - planting the rhyming style firmly back at its roots.

The themes inside range from poems about seasons, pets and summer holidays to odes and dedications to friends and families. This anthology brings the fun of rhyming poetry back for good and will hopefully entertain for years to come.

Steve Twelvetree
Editor

CONTENTS

DEATH TRAIN

We were locked into the carriage,
On that train in dark Peru,
The guide had said: 'Be careful,
There are bandits after you.'

The blinds were pulled down ready,
The windows all tight shut,
Waiting for the whistle,
The guard in his tin hut.

The wheels they were a-moving,
Heavy on the track,
Our hearts they were a-pounding,
There was no turning back.

They said this train was robbed each day,
We kept our money close,
Tight in our belts, next to our skin,
An invite not to pose.

We were on our way to Cuzco,
The highlight of our trip,
Where llamas walked and Incas talked,
Used stones instead of brick.

We finally arrived there,
Alive and in one piece,
To wonder at the sights there,
High cold, I wore my fleece.

Linda Lawrence

THE YORKSHIRE MINERS

I remember the old man sitting on the bench
Telling us such stories of old,
Children would gather from far and wide
To hear tales of a different world.

He came from a family of miners
Who dug coal from the bowels of the earth,
Often their job was very hard
Yet it was bred in them from birth.

Our eyes were glued to this old man,
With surprise at the tales he would tell,
Of pit ponies who never saw daylight
Down the coal shaft much deeper than wells.

He told us about a fire in the pit,
And of the men who couldn't get out,
He brought memories back of that day long ago,
I knew what he was talking about.

I was one of the kids who was crying,
Waiting for signs at the pit head,
I had a special reason to wait -
Down that pit were my brother and my dad.

Vera Ewers

SONNET FOR HOMEWORK

Where do I find those fourteen lines to rhyme?
The task is set and I must play my part.
Had I but world enough, the wit and time,
I would produce *such* specimens of art!

But Shakespeare, Donne, and Milton came before,
To follow them is little more than joke.
What is the sonnet's heart, what is its core
Of meanings wrapped and trapped inside the cloak

Of structure strict, pentameters, set rhymes?
Feeling stockaded by a fence of rules,
In this tough exercise, let me commit no crimes,
Nor hear the shudders of the ancient schools

Of sonneteers, who tossed them with an air -
I simply stitch what very soon will tear.

Julie Longman

SONNET

Diverse indeed the talents within our hands,
The deft, the gentle, fingers that can make
A garment from a mass of twisted strands,
Fashion a silver goblet - or a cake.
Gnarled they may be, stubby, square and strong,
Slim and elegant, work-worn, wrinkled, dry
Yet from a 'cello they may charm a song,
Paint a portrait, still an infant's cry.
Outstretched in friendly greeting or farewell,
Thrusting a spade deep into crumbling earth,
Proffering a chalice, pulling on a bell,
Tending the dying, assisting at a birth.
And hands clasped in affection may transmit
The skill of loving - and the pain of it.

Meryl Docker

PAST ECHOES

Researching family history with dedicated zeal
Means hours of patient searching which will hopefully reveal -
All sorts of strange encounters with ones we never knew,
Providing avid interest tracking down each clue.
Sometimes disappointment when the wrong path we have taken
But then jubilation when the jigsaw bits are shaken -
And into our researches another link recorded
The chain a little longer and patience well rewarded.
Sometimes a special name stands out tho' centuries divide,
The name becomes a person and our hearts are filled with pride,
To think we share the kith and kin and carry on their name,
Though in their day that name may have no accolade to fame
I have an ancestor like this, who fills my thoughts with praise,
I think he was a humble man who worked hard all his days.
A mariner of many years who served his country well,
In Nelson's fleet Trafalgar braved and faced the guns of Hell.
With Christian faith and Christian hope one day I hope we'll meet,
Upon God's green and pleasant land where life becomes complete,
And we shall have eternity upon that glorious shore,
To share our thoughts in perfect peace and open memories' door.
So all unanswered questions will then be laid to rest,
The jigsaw all assembled and a perfect end of quest.

Patricia Ruffle

SUNSETS AND SUNRISES

The daylight is fading away, the sky is all ablaze
With the fiery red glow of the sun's dying rays,
Streaked here and there with a clear turquoise blue,
Whilst the edges of the clouds are tinted a pinkish hue.
The pink changes to purple before my wondering eyes
As the last light of the sun leaves our darkening skies.
Sunrises and sunsets are glorious sights to see,
Such beauty I perceive in the silhouette of a tree:
Their traceries of twigs stretching across the sky
Forming an intricate pattern so pleasing to the eye.
And as I watch the light slowly fading from the skies
I wonder about the lands where the sun is about to rise.

Christine Naylor

HE WAS MY HERO!

He didn't realise he was so small,
And nothing escaped his steely stare.
He was a tough little character, pompous and proud,
Who sent people scurrying, in fear and despair.

He was our guard dog in miniature
Alert and hostile,
Who patrolled his domain,
With cunning and guile.

He was a joy, he was loving,
But to strangers, savage!
He would lunge with fury,
And trousers ravage!

He'd growl, he'd snarl,
He was my lightweight friend.
I adored him, I spoiled him,
My love knew no end.

He was delightful, devoted,
A real *Superstar.*
He was really quite small,
Our long-haired . . . *Chihuahua.*

Ann White

INDOOR BOWLS

My wood begins its silent trip towards the distant jack,
But almost instantly I wish that I could have it back!
I've taken insufficient green or failed the weight to measure.
My Skip's expression shows my wood has failed to give him pleasure.

And then I have to stand and watch as my opponent draws,
Concealing my impatience as his wood attracts applause.
I fail to keep my cool as I survey his chalky kiss,
And in a reckless moment my next wood I fire - and miss!

My Skip's reaction says it all: he's far from being complacent,
Especially when the next wood up is once again adjacent.
And so I take my final wood, resisting violent glory,
And finish nestling on the jack - an entirely different story.

Thank goodness it was triples: that I had that extra chance
To pass my Skip in middle rink and meet his cheerful glance.
Perhaps we'll still not win the game - no reason why we should -
But all this evening I can dream about my perfect wood!

John Eldridge

RIDE FOREVER

Here I am riding along
shaking my head to my favourite song
people look on and think we are crazy
people look on they think we are lazy
they think we don't work to earn a day's pay.
It's a hypocritical attitude of people today.
Ignore the bigots they don't understand
in metal boxes they roam the land.
We ride in a group, people call us a gang
we like to party and go out with a bang!
Some are not so dedicated they won't ride in the rain
some ride in all conditions and don't complain.
People ask why, we just like the freedom
people ask where, all over this great Kingdom.
Engine a-thumping along with the others
riding along with the Biking brothers.
Ride free and ride together
Ride safe and ride forever.

J E Royle

A WHISPER AWAY

Iron-red the copper beeches sigh
The great oaks sprawl against the sky,
Stray breezes bless dreamtime with lips rose-red
And all my senses are led
To where hope of peace brushes my mind as it passes
This way making happiness only a dream away.
Nylon-soft the stream glides
A lingering ripple at the water's margin hides
In the quivering grasses.
Calm of quiet moment fingers emotion to say
Peace is only a whisper away.
Breaking ocean waves
Rush ashore to flood secret caves,
Sea winds kiss the rocky shore,
A promise falls on this world unshadowed grey
And peace is no more
Than a whisper away.

Pat Isiorho

SEX DISCRIMINATION

A woman's work is never done
and in my life there's not much fun.
The day is full of woe and strife
for I am only someone's wife.

Each morning dawns and cloths I bleach
so this request I do beseech.
Please do not let me wear a frown
when evening comes and cloths are brown!

I wash the pots and pans all day
and ne'er a drop flies off astray
but messy men drive me insane
with showers on the windowpane.

There're whiskers in the bathroom too
and wellies needed in the loo
with half the garden in the hall
why do we want a man at all?

Phenomenons attract to me
for in my house I'm stuck with three.
I love them but I can't pretend
They drive me slowly round the bend!

When first your love he tries to win
he'll use his charm to haul you in
within his net, he'll you ensnare
then snore forever in his chair!

Daughter, sister, mother and wife,
please tell me there's another life
where I can wander wild and free,
somewhere where I can be just *me!*

Jill Barker

A Visitor

As I came home one afternoon
In springtime sunshine warm,
Saw buds that opened into bloom,
Displaying all their charm,
I bent, to pick Veronica
Out from the grass so green.
Had I not picked Veronica,
I never would have seen
        My little guest.

Oh yes, I had a visitor
Right there, out on my lawn.
I never would have thought of him,
When I went out this morn.
A little ball of brown on green,
Still cold, but getting warm;
Awakening from winter sleep.
Springtime was his alarm.
        My little guest.

I went and got a little bowl
With meaty cat food moist,
And put it right in front of him.
His little heart rejoiced.
Slowly, the prickly ball uncurled
And made straight for the food.
And I stood back and watched and smiled.
Oh yes, it tasted good.
        My little guest - a hedgehog.

Helga Dharmpaul

I Don't Believe It

Went skiing but it didn't snow
Made a blind date, she didn't show
Got in the bath, the telephone rang
Changed a fuse and it went bang!

Set the video on the wrong channel
Soap in my eyes, couldn't find the flannel
Went out for the day, caught the wrong train
Forgot my umbrella, got soaked in the rain.

Got seasick although the sea was calm
Someone stole my burglar alarm.
Found a ten-pound note in the mud
Yes, you're right, it was a dud!

Lost my girl to my best friend
Injured my back and couldn't bend.
Broke my key in the lock
My electric razor gave me a shock!

My trousers split as I knelt to pray
Sat on a chair but it gave way.
My car brakes failed going down a hill
Forgot to pay my council tax bill!
What else can happen, I really don't know
Can anything make my confidence grow?

Norman Desmond Humphreys

FAMILIES

What would we do without our families
To cherish and to tend
The housework and the washing
And all the things to mend?
We wash them and we feed them
And brush their tangled hair
Make sure they get to school on time
With nice clean clothes to wear
When their lessons finish
It's straight back home at three
They know they won't go hungry
Mum is there to make the tea
Not long before they reach them
Those dreaded teenage years
With moods and slanging matches
Through waves of love and tears
Then, yet again, they fall I love
And soon they fly the nest
You help them with the wedding
And try to do your best
Then, when they have their little ones
And you're enjoying a well-earned rest
They want to go out and have some fun
So you know what's coming next
Just when you thought you could relax
After years of joy and pain
They say 'Oh Nan will babysit'
And the circle starts again.

Anne Tarbox

A BALANCE KEPT

Moon in the east, sun in the west;
The coloured clouds lie soft, between;
The distant woods are dulled with mist;
The nearby fields are green.

A disc of pearl and a copper disc;
The mist has married the clouds, like smoke;
The blades of the winter wheat stand clean;
The bracken dies by the road.

The moon has risen, the sun has slipped;
The changing light, by fine degrees,
Thins out the sky; the rooks draw close
To roost like fruit in the winter trees.

Odd, how the light-deserted sky
Glows for a moment yet more bright -
Grows whiter, larger, as you watch . . .
While all the roads silt up with night.

Judy Hindley

A RONDEAU

I loved you then in distant days,
Before the flood, before the rays
Of heaven's fire had scorched the land,
Turning forests to desert sand
Where only the unwary strays.

When quinqueremes sought foreign bays,
Ploughing the seas' uncharted ways,
Guided by Neptune's unseen hand,
I loved you then.

When Golden Hordes made long forays
With blazon shields and swords ablaze,
Travelling east as they had planned
To seek the road to Samarkand,
I looked at you with steadfast gaze
And loved you then.

Celia G Thomas

ONCE UPON A DREAM!

Look up at the sky, and tell me,
What do you see?
Do you think you could find out there
A reflection of me?

Look beyond the clouds so fair!
Past the Milky Way.
Could I possibly be out there?
Somewhere far, far away!

Far beyond the universe;
Where the naked eye, can't see!
Do you think that there could be
A facsimile of me?

Way across the stratosphere,
Where no mortal's ever been
I'm sure that I have been there,
Once upon a dream!

Richard Ninnis

BETTER TIMES

Poetry in simple form
Is coming back to be the 'norm'.
I can't abide this modern stuff
When nothing flows; I've had enough
Of current trends; too weird by half!
(It's not supposed to make you laugh)
Take drama, music, so-called 'art',
You can't tell which is end or start.
I hope this odd ode scans and rhymes.
Now, drink a toast to 'Better times'.

Corinne Lovell

SUMMERTIME

Summertime is like a breath of fresh air,
It is too short to stand and stare -
Waiting for something to happen, to grow,
Where does all our valuable time go?

The flowers are already open, in bloom,
Is there any time, any room, for more to appear,
It is halfway through the year -
Soon autumn will be here.

Sunbathing, swimming in the sea,
Children laughing, shouting with glee,
Barbecues, picnics, ice-cream, cream teas,
Are all part of summer for you and me.

Walking, riding, seeing the views,
Taking time out to pick and choose -
Evenings together, to see the land.
Its breathtaking beauty, serenity, so grand.

Yet summer can be a middling thing.
Not a definite season, just months in-between,
To go on holidays, to finish chores,
The little things that usually are a bore.

Painting the house, washing curtains and nets,
Doing the gardening, taking pets to the vets -
For their annual de-fleaing, while the carpets get cleaned
This is my view of the summer scene.

You could say I'm a bit of a bore,
When comes the time of the summer chores,
Give me the autumn, when things start to change.
Colours mingling, rearranged for a new season to begin.

Susan Askew

POETRY RECALLED

I love the sound of poetry
The rhythmic ebb and flow
Of well-remembered cadences
From verse of long ago

Words can prove so powerful
However we may feel
May sadden or amuse us
Inspire us with their zeal

Poems taught as infants
We memorised by rote
Progressing then to poetry
With famous lines we quote

The poignant words that linger
Composed in World War One
The words of Poet Laureates
Of Shakespeare and John Donne

The legacy they left us
The test of time has stood
We wander still with Wordsworth
And smile with Thomas Hood.

Sheila J Leheup

NOT A POEM?

'This isn't a poem, how can it be,
when I can understand every word,
and it actually rhymes, you see,
now that is totally absurd!

What's more, in line four, you say 'joy',
you must learn to be less direct,
disconnect from the hoi polloi,
we must keep this craft select.

The rhythm should never be so clear,
or your meaning so bluntly rendered,
clichés like 'sweet love' or 'black fear'
are too easily remembered.

'Golden daffodils', what a cliché!
so everyone loves it - so what!
Such food for the soul is passé,
new poets use a different pot.

To stay elite, follow this plan,
never try to communicate,
or satisfy the common man,
serve him with a half-empty plate.

Cover your true thoughts, hide
them in mental aspic jelly,
like nouvelle cuisine that feeds pride,
but still leaves an empty belly.'

Gwen V Lewis

THE DAWN

The splendour of the colours
as the sun rose from its sleep,
The heavenly glow in the sky
Is a memory you'll want to keep.

Have *you* seen the beauty of a sunrise?
It's a joy too good to miss,
The beginning of a new day
Beckons you - get up - and don't delay.

The air is fresh and bracing
Everything smells so sweet
Soon the fumes from traffic
Will spoil that lovely treat.

The birds are busy looking
For their morning feed,
And the squirrels come down from the trees
To see what they can steal.

They chase away the blue tits
That are pecking at the nuts
But up against the squirrels
The birds don't stand a chance.

Even the pigeons
Find they can't get a meal
And must return later
When the squirrels have had their fill.

The noise is getting louder,
Another day has begun,
Soon children will be out playing
And having lots of fun.

Laura D Harris

THE END IS NIGH

New year again, another year past,
And we're all here again,
As we look back on time we lost,
Wishing we could stop the pain.

We look all around this earth,
And see it's looking grim,
As another woman is giving birth,
But its future's looking dim.

Mugging, rape and high speed chases,
Splashed over the local paper,
Homeless poverty and race against races,
It'll all stop sooner than later.

By then what will be left, I ask,
For all our future generations,
The earth will be like the Grim Reaper's mask
Nations fighting nations.

One day someone will come and then,
The bells will toll aloud,
To press the button and say 'Amen',
The earth gone in a puff of cloud.

Kim Chadwick

MARRIAGE

November the fourth, is so near,
Life will change, but nothing to fear.
It's the start of our new life,
The day you will become my wife.

I can't wait for this day to come,
When at long last, we'll be joined as one.
Life for us will be love and bliss,
And it all began, with a simple kiss.

I just want to let you know,
My care and love will always grow.
Even though we will be wed,
It doesn't mean that love is dead.

The love we have is far too strong,
We've waited for this for so long.
Very soon the world will see,
Marriage to you was meant to be.

Ewan

POETRY'S LOVELY WORDS

Lovely words complied together
Like petals of a pretty flower
Comfort to a heart distressed
To a tormented mind a lubricant
Sense of laughter, sense of song
Around a glowing fire's singalong
A precious gift worth more than gold
Lovely words the mind unfolds
Releasing pleasures to a world disturbed
Simple words no need to beguile
Remembering the innocent mind of a child
God inspired that mind with wealth untold
Selected words from the mind's vocabulary stored
On loan, for a time to society
Do we give enough praise
Or try to comprehend
The artists with brush?
The poet with pen?

Often into small hours of the night
The artist still paints
The poet still writes.

F Gibson

FIFTY YEARS

(Susan)

When you were born fifty years ago
Such a beloved and lovely child
You quickly reached the age of four
And you used to drive me wild

You'd bring hedgehogs into the house
Drop frogs on to my lap
Then climb the tree for apples
When I tried to take a nap

At the age of five you rushed from school
Shouting aloud with glee
'Mum, I've been chosen to be Mary'
In the Christmas nativity.'

The years passed by, you married
Then had children of your own
Now you've reached the age of fifty
My! How the time has flown.

J Jones

MAY 2000

As grains of sand thro' the hands of children at play
So the summer of promises slips quickly away
Early May tiptoed in, bringing hours of sun
Whispering tales of the pleasures and joys yet to come
Now the calendar tells us days are hurrying past
Faithless June and July, cloudy, grey, overcast,
Yet, to come, there is August, September, will they
Renew all the promises made so blithely by May?

Maybe!

G Halliwell

SEA TALK

I like to walk upon the beach
my mind can wander out of reach
it mingles with the sand and sea
there's nothing there to worry me.
The sea tells tales of ancient times
singing songs and chanting rhymes
whispering secrets from deep in its swell
knowing things that only time can tell.
Whatever the weather I feel free to go
wherever I want to it's somewhere I know
with the wind in my face I feel calm and free
it's a place where I'm welcome to think about me . . .

Wendy Blundell

MAX AND THE MOUNTAIN PONIES

A strong Welsh cob was Max, my horse
For working and riding. He was, of course,
Not highly bred and expensive like my horses before
When I lived in England, which I had to insure.
Max was fast and reliable, not lazy, not slow.
Bought at the West Wales horse sale, some years ago.

Rode over the mountain on him one day.
The sound of his hoof beats made wild ponies neigh.
From near and far distance on still morning air
Came voices of gelding, stallion and mare.
Max hailed them back, and the mountains were ringing,
Just as though all the horses were singing.
A unique experience I'll never forget
The memory of that morning stays with me yet.

Laura Föst

A Villanelle To Dawn

Sweet song of birds proclaims the death of night.
Weak rays of sun herald the dawn of day.
The whole world stirs in turn with the growing light.

The dull red orb is changed to gleaming bright.
God-fearing people kneel at their beds to pray.
Sweet song of birds proclaims the death of night.

The blindness caused by dark is changed to sight
And children's fears the shining beams allay.
The whole world stirs in turn with growing light.

To wake sound sleepers shrill alarms incite
While weary workers plod with clods of clay
Sweet song of birds proclaims the death of night.

All forms of life thrive in warmth of sun's might
Sent down to Earth with every blinding ray
The whole world stirs in turn with growing light.

So day by day, black darkness is vanquished quite.
Revolving Earth within its path will stay.
Sweet song of birds proclaims the death of night
The whole world stirs in turn with growing light.

Hywel Davies

POETRY AND PROSE

To educate is, in its broadest sense,
development of personality
in individuals, and in furtherance
of knowledge, stored for all posterity;
accumulated wisdom, we must pass
each generation, ever forward brought,
developing the character and nous
of those of us receptive to be taught.
The thirst for knowledge, betterment and skill,
vocational, high-tech or cultural,
with many never wanes as they mature;
their impetus demands that they excel.
For such, good poetry and prose will teach
them all the parts that other crafts can't reach.

Christopher Head

LET US LOOK AT THE DOME . . .

When it's ceased to be the home
Of that incompetent NMEC.

They do not appear to see
That it is a pit without
Any base. Money flows out
Never to be found again.

Financiers, they strain
For *one* reason to give more.
Here's a way for it to score!

I have read there is enough
Room inside for sporting stuff,
Like football pitches, or athletic tracks,

If that *circus* gets the axe.
Let's invite runners to train,
And check times in each lane.

We could breed new sporting 'greats',
Winning at undreamed-of rates,
When we had abandoned hope.
They won't need speed-pills or dope.

Gillian C Fisher

I'VE GOT MY BUS PASS IN MY HAND

From child to soldier bathed in mother's tears.
From warrior father's mould a hero cast
to serve in north of Scotland, stripping gears.
It's hard to think some fifty years have passed
in dull kaleidoscope of rush-hour years,
the crushing weight of work-a-daily task
and taste of ageing unemployment's fears.
So I have watched a listless life flush past
but now I've got my bus pass in my hands.

Now I'll kill time on my Retirement Watch;
throw out alarm clocks, visit foreign lands,
buy pants 'two inches more from waist to crotch'
and change my paper pounds for golden rands.
I'll buy myself a better class of Scotch,
and strut my stuff on Caribbean sands
and, striking lucky, carve a youthful notch:
deny I own a bus pass out of hand.

Swept on to lies by smug suburban sighs
I shall describe exotic moonflower leis
at weekend golf - such healthy exercise,
and soundly sleep at end of fleet-foot days.

Alan Chesterfield

MRS SHAKESPEARE 2000

Washing dancing on the line,
Fresh from out the tub,
But there's still the ironing to do . .
Aye! There's the rub!

Mixing flour with egg and milk,
It's Yorkshire pud for tea!
Will it rise all crispy-light . . .?
To be or not to be!

A crumbling tooth (the last I own!)
The dentist's chair tomorrow.
She'll have to yank the rotter out . . .
Parting is such sweet sorrow.

A cigarette burn on the rug,
A guilty-looking male,
'I'll give them up tomorrow, Luv . . .'
(And thereby hangs a tale!)

Lottery ticket in the bin,
Still haven't won a bean!
Have a drink and go to bed . . .
To sleep, perchance to dream!

Sally Thompson

THE CARLISLE TO SETTLE LINE

It is said to be one of the loveliest routes
Of our network of railway tracks,
And those of us who travel it have no doubt
That for sheer beauty it nothing lacks.

We see boundless acres of fertile green vales
And vast moorland, so rugged and wild,
And in the background standing guard o'er the dales
Are the Pennines, like a mother with her child.

There are stately viaducts crossing deep wide rifts
And dark tunnels hewn from solid rock;
All these were built with man's tenacity and grit.
Hard to comprehend; very hard to take stock.

A plaque in a churchyard nestling under the line
Commemorates this arduous feat,
And this serves us all as an everlasting sign
That none who travel will ever forget.

That it be built high up was society's decree,
To cause no disturbance to folk below,
Which is why these panoramic views are ours to see;
The toll its building took is ours to know.

Marlene Allen

Somerly Park

Oh little Lesser Celandine
on smudgy soil you greenly grow.
Your petals are shaped spring sunshine
March nipped, but mirrored yellow
in new daylight that streams through this
empty wood. The beam bright cries out
encaptured by your soul. Promise
warm heady leaves and days. No doubt
blossoms, bee's lazy ways. And there
shadows sweet with birdsong. But you
will quietly sleep hidden still where
your brave prelude called to one who
for dreaming summers does not care.

Richard Jones

JUST FOR TUPPENCE

Just for tuppence I could buy,
A staircase leading to the sky,
I would climb right up just to see
If the man in the moon looked like me.

For tuppence more I could get
A great big green fishing net,
At the river's edge I'd sit all day,
And catch the one that got away.

I could if I'm lucky buy a car
And travel countries near and far,
I'd see the world and all that's in it
And be back home in just a minute.

If only I had tuppence
There's so much I could do,
Instead I've just one penny
And I'm giving that to you.

Georgina Waite

THE APPLE TREE

I started off a sapling close to a garden wall
Almost hidden by the flowers - I really was quite small
But by these I was protected when those icy winds did blow
And with the help of sun and showers I soon began to grow.

During the winter months the nights are cold and long
At dawn the silence broken by a chorus of birdsong
Then many lovely flowers showed us spring was on its way
With all their pretty colours that help brighten every day.

I could feel my branches stretching upwards to the sky
Watching the birds and butterflies, how I wish that I could fly
I then found I was covered with new leaves everywhere
And such beautiful blossom whose fragrance fills the air.

By summer my roots were planted so firmly in the ground
And I heard someone mention - no nicer apples to be found
Soon it will be autumn when my leaves will start to fall
But I'll be back next spring just as sturdy - strong and tall.

Mary Lunn

CORTINA

Shaking craggy heads free of winter's shroud,
  The aged Dolomites, their faces raise,
From dizzy heights, they loom, thro' clearing cloud,
  To the warmth of the sun's strengthening rays.

Cotton wool overhangs on every roof,
  Have disappeared, on those first days of spring -
No longer seen, the pony's flying hoof,
  Pulling the sleigh, whose bell, has ceased to ring.

Not now, the scrape of swift skis, in the street -
  The walls of snow, one morning, are no more.
There's song, where cataract and river meet -
  Far distant now, the torrent's angry roar.

Into the pool, melts the frozen fountain -
  Gone for a season, its prison of ice.
Now, fresh green, are the slopes of the mountain,
  Where soon, will wake the sleeping edelweiss.

Elizabeth Harris

OSCAR

Oscar is a poodle with a wide enchanting smile.
He is the best companion and that by many a mile,
    He has his faults despite his grin;
    He's rather fat instead of thin
    which could become a trial.

He likes to take the newspaper each morning from the door
but cannot carry it too far and drops it on the floor:
    his teeth have left him in a fix
    because he has but five (not six)
    within his bottom jaw.

He often sleeps too soundly and then wakes up with a start
which make him go all wobbly, as if he'd got a 'heart'.
    We must accept his awful fits
    which scare each one of us to bits
    as of him it's a part.

He's handsome and entirely black with long and silky ears,
but they were full of wax you know, which every owner fears.
    The vet said that he'd have to chop;
    that meant poor Oscar had an op.
    which left us all in tears.

Although we paid a lot for him to take him to a show
and make of him a Champion for everyone to know -
    he'll always be our pride and joy;
    for he is like our little boy,
    but it's a bitter blow.

We thought he'd win and gain for us our fortune and our fame
but we have had to rethink this, accepting how he came.
    You see he's always such a friend.
    We'd rather have him in the end.
    We love him just the same.

Janet Miller

I BELIEVE IN YOU
(For Danielle Marie)

Do you believe in fairy tales of pretty ballerina girls,
With fairy wings and butterflies and golden shiny curls?
Do you believe in angels of flowing lace and white,
Smiling faces, long blonde hair, so dainty in their flight?
Do you believe in princesses with beautiful long gowns,
Flowers in their hair, glitter on their faces and never wear a frown?
Do you believe in Cinderella and the story of the ball,
A plain girl made so pretty, she was the belle of them all,
If you are a little girl, I know you'll answer yes,
If you are a little boy, your belief will be far less,
Because all little girls believe in pretty, magical things,
Of fairies, flowers, ladybirds and shiny silver rings,
The nice things in this world are all things that are true,
So carry on believing but most of all believe in you -

Kelly Pidwell

A Plea For Rhyme

Some think that rhyme's a lot of froth -
I hope I shan't incur their wrath
And be condemned as hopeless Goth.

Yet in the shapeless free verse broth
Let's try to weigh more than a moth:
The public don't have ears of cloth.

Don't make of rhyme a Behemoth,
Or see technique as harsh sackcloth -
And half rhyme's there in case of sloth.

Anne Sanderson

ONCE IN A WHILE

(To the girl who has probably forgotten me)

I wonder if now I'm no longer there,
Very occasionally, once in a while,
You remember the boy who used to stare
Lovingly at you with a far-off smile,
And blushing when it was kindly return'd.
Do you ever wonder where he has gone?
Did you ever guess he secretly yearn'd
To hold and kiss you, and spent nights forlorn,
Despising himself for not telling you
His true feelings. But now it's far too late,
And I doubt I'll find another girl who
Moves me like you. I lament my sad fate
Of spending my life without your warm smile,
Please think of that boy, just once in a while.

Martin Foreman

WILLY THE WEASEL

Willy the weasel,
Stood at his easel,
For a portrait he had painted,
Of Cyril the stoat,
In his winter coat,
With whom he was acquainted,
If you look closely you can determine,
The cut of his fine trim ermine,
Beneath it he wrote,
'To a very good stoat
My friend and trustee
Mentor and Bon-Ami
Can you come to tea on Monday the first?
We'll eat rabbits until we burst.'
Cyril replied in verse
Though it was rather cutting and terse,
'My heart is filled with sorrow,
For I can't come to tea be it today or tomorrow,
For the farmer has dug a new furrow
And has cleft a big hole in my burrow,
So I'm sure you'll agree,
I simply can't come to tea,
Be it today or tomorrow!'

Alan Pow

Salute To Calgary Mull

There is a croft across the sea,
Where ancient Macs were glad to be.
Where Donald, Angus, and their ilk
Could grow the wool as soft as silk.
Where Chrissie, Nessie, and their kind
Could twirl a wheel and really wind
The cloth, the old plaid long since hidden.

There is a croft, deserted now,
No crossbred cur, no island cow,
No wee 'uns cry, no lassies clack,
Donald is na'e coming back.
Down by the pier no vessel rides,
Just seaweed sliding on the tides.
This place of Scots long ridden.

There is a croft we cannot spy
In far-off lands, 'neath many a sky,
In continents and countries new
The Macs still flourish strong and true.
Not settlements of twa-roomed shacks
But picket fence for front and backs,
Wide stairs, big rooms, twa cars, na'e midden.

Denis Pentlow

BABY

For nine months he hides away,
as you await that special day,
into the world comes a bundle of joy,
is it a girl, or is it a boy?

Ten tiny fingers and ten tiny toes,
big blue eyes and a little button nose,
so perfectly formed is this little one,
now his life has just begun!

As the days go by, and the more he grows,
he's getting so big, he's outgrown his clothes.
Now he can crawl and is trying to walk,
look out for the day he starts to talk!

For toilet training the time has come,
a few find it easy, but it's harder for some
he'll soon go to school and make lots of friends,
but your job as his mother just never ends!

Christine Jane Bennett

FELINE SUPERIORITY

Aloof and golden-pawed I sit
upon the fence, to avoid the grit
that is intended, this I know,
to resurface the pavement there below.

Like a cat on a hot tin roof I tread
along the nail-topped fence instead
to where, beneath, the landing's plain,
when I with dignity may stroll again.

A gauging eye, a silent jump -
Ah good, I missed that awful rubbish dump;
those humans, *so* uncouth, I find,
whilst I, the cat, leave only cleanliness behind.

A frequent wash, all undisturbed,
disperse the fleas, their actions curbed;
with grace and poise I strut my stuff,
disdaining contact with the feral scruff.

From vantage points above the ground
I watch and listen, alert to sound
from prey or foe that come in range,
including humans - they're *very* strange!

Aloof and golden-pawed I squat
upon the neighbouring fence - 'That's not
allowed, puss,' so I'm told:
'Shoo, get down, you're far too bold,'

Like a green-eyed monster off I speed
to give illusion I've paid good heed,
but very soon I regain my stance
with aplomb and dignity - and chance!

Ann Voaden

FIFTY PLUS CONFIDENCE

Isn't it sad, I wish I had the confidence before,
To do the things that others had,
To use the whole dance floor.

But there I sat like a wallflower,
Watching the other kids twirl,
Wishing that *I* could find the power,
To show them how *I* could swirl.

Not daring to show my best at school
Afraid to stretch up my hand.
Frightened I might look an awful fool
If conspicuously asked to stand.

Oh! How I feel so cheated
I let my youth slip by
If only life could be repeated,
I'd reach up for the sky.

Take what life has to offer,
Learn to swim and jive.
Now I crave more adventure,
Get what I can out of life.

For now I find at fifty plus,
My confidence at its peak.
Take life by the horns I must
So if I want to speak, I'll speak.

I've left it a little late it's true
I need to make up for lost time.
I wish I'd done what I wanted to do
In the negative years of my prime
But of all the triumphs I faltered,
      I'm determined to conquer a few.

A M Wilson

THE TEST OF RHYME

Through generations it has stood the test of time,
The traditional, familiar nursery rhyme,
By youngsters easily remembered off by heart,
Teaching vocabulary an essential part.

Unrhyming poetry, even if meaningful,
Is soon forgotten, unlike the traditional.
Rhyme and rhythm make up the lyrics of a song:
In our society they will always belong.

That is what poetry for most is all about,
Sentences that end in rhyme from pages shout.
This simple form of verse can then be expanded
By adults and children they will be demanded.

When poetry rhymes it will be understood,
Which can only serve to do literary good.
If readers are interested, they may progress,
To alternate forms of poetry digress.

So then, let us keep rhyming poetry alive,
Maintaining readers', writers' interest to survive.
Once the imagination is triggered, then caught,
Other forms of poetry will be studied, sought.

Janet Hewitt

STROLL AT EVENTIME

Distantly at the woodland's edge
Where leafy glade gives way to sedge
And water meadows green and lush
Lie silent in the dusky hush,
To amble pensively and slow
All at peace in the afterglow
By the side of a placid stream
Enchanted by this evening dream.

So silently encroaching night
Devours remnants of sunset's flight
Now passing to the horizon's rim
Obscures the sun so pale, so dim.
A final shaft of golden light
Flashes skywards into the night
And nestling in the velvety dim
Pale moon projects her luminous rim.

B Wilson

RUSH HOUR ON THE UNDERGROUND

The Central line, the Central line
All aboard for the Central line
Like sardines in a tin we pack
Hard to breathe back to back
Down into the tunnel deep
Tiger roaring, cannot sleep
Churning thro' with quickening pace
Ever onward, ever race
At last emerging into light
Banging, clanging, holding tight
Stretching, straining, feeling sore
Squeeze thro' people to the door
Till my weary thoughts unwind
Leave the monster far behind
Leave the monster far behind
Leave
    the
        monster
            far
                behind!

Gladys Llewellyn

MANSIONS

Mum, I'm beginning to look just *like* you
    And say the things you used to say
And now that I know you were right all along
    It gets harder every day.

When I look in the mirror I see your dear face
    And the smile I see is your own
My hair's going silver in just the same way
    As yours when we both lived at home.

Sometimes in the street, I'll see someone's back
    And the hair and the coat are the same
But when they turn round it's somebody else
    And I have to hold back my blame!

It's a *selfish* love that cries out in its hurt
    And would have you return again
For Heaven has wiped away all your tears
    And recompensed you for all your pain.

Far better to be in your Father's House
    In His Mansions sumptuous and wide
And talk with the long-lost friends of your youth
    Who preceded you into the light.

'How *like* her you are!' the neighbours all say
    And their words are like salve to my sores
But I'll *never* match up to your *own* golden soul
    No matter how long my life's course.

Shirley Dyer

MISERABLE

Perched on perching branch high,
The crows head towards the threatening sky,
Their telephone-like bleeping voices
Not chose too listen to, by chorus,
Pitching tones, calling the rain to come.
Rain clouds, soon black out the sun.

Mid-morning, way into the afternoon
A deluge like monsoon.
An April shower,
Lasting many hours,
Miserable sheep huddled in groups.
Damp chickens, cooped up in their coops.

Cows feeding in the plush fields,
Eating wet pasture meals.
Feeling miserable wrapped in sodden furs.
No shelter under the lofty firs.
No end to the prolonged shower.
Sunshine the wish of the hour.

Miserable and forlorn.
Cursing the day one was born.
But, they are still,
Primroses in the hedgerows, on the hill.
Shoes squelching, treading wet.
To the primroses, the rain poses no threat.

Wet grumbling miserable crows,
Listen instead to the birds in the hedgerows.
Their song, not of complain.
Rain or shine, to them every day's the same.
No one loves a thorny thorn
World will awake to a new April morn.

B G Clarke

LOVE IS

Love is a feeling beyond compare
Love is showing that you care
Love is being ready to share
Love is always being there

Love is oh so loyal and true
Love is being kind to you
Love is ready to start anew
Love is giving what is due

Love is forever so designed
Love is to be gentle not unkind
Love is what you always find
Love is sure never to mind

Love is not trying self to please
Love is never a harmful tease
Love is not looking just to seize
Love is all about you not me

Love is not a windy gust
Love is nothing to do with lust
Love is built on lasting trust
Love is pure this is a must

Love is feelings deep inside
Love is a smile you cannot hide
Love is nothing to do with pride
Love is not to be denied

Love is longer than a first date
Love is something that cannot wait
Love is a happy contented state
Love is finding a lifelong mate

Love is singing in the rain
Love is causing joy not pain
Love is not seeking selfish gain
Love is here and will remain

Dennis Whittaker

TESTING TIME

Time is a gift with the gift of life,
We're inclined to take both for granted
                              when all seems right,
We don't stop to take stock or look deep inside,
Life is for living and time is on our side.

Our parents take control when we are young,
We accept their guidance, we need their love,
Then we seek total freedom to do as we please,
So don't hold us back, we need you to agree.

Just to know that you care and we can come home,
The key in our pocket gets very warm,
When we need reassurance from family love,
We know we'll be welcomed as nowhere else could.

And as we grow up a day at a time,
Making mistakes then coming back into line,
We can see for ourselves, what it takes to mature,
Our values are placed in an order that's sure.

Kathleen McBurney

THE HEALTHY OPTION, OR, 'SALAD DAZE'!

No salt - no fat.
No this - no that.
Will life become a bore?
To live to eat
Or eat to live?
No thought of *that* before.
Had better try
To bypass *'Fry'* -
Just grill and boil and steam.
It might be hard
To give up lard
And butter, cheese and cream.
No cakes to make
No pies to bake
All suet *'puds'* omit.
With time to spare
Walk here - walk there -
Will *soon* be fighting fit!

Joanna Hearth

SPAIN

When me and my friends went to Spain
We ate and drank on the plane.
When we got there
I decided to wash my hair.
Then we went to the bar
And then we hired a car
To see the sights of Spain
And then it began to rain.

Emma Perfect

A Rough Guide To . . . Extractions!

The dentist said what she knew
And told me her view
That most of my teeth should come out;
She'd refer me to hospital for everyone's sake
Visualising the blood my inflamed gums would make.

The Consultant was kind
And in order to find
The ones that needed to go
Sent me for X-rays which he then showed to me
So the ones that he chose I could readily see.

My next appointment was six weeks ahead
For the operation itself, he said;
It would take that time for my dentist's impressions
To be made into dentures which he would then seat
In my mouth, post-extractions, to make it look neat.

On the appointed day I checked in at seven
Had the 'op' before ten and was 'round' by eleven;
For sickness and pain came a jab and a pill
But even from my gums *no blood* did appear
So if *you* need this treatment, you've nothing to fear!

Marjory Scott

THE LETTER BOX

We have lived in *1, Elm Grove,* for fifteen years.
There was one thing that I noticed
And I gave three hearty cheers,
For just across the road
Quite close to our abode
Was the very thing that everybody needs.
Some people come from near or far
Just walking or by car,
If it rains they have to run
Surely that is not much fun
To put their letters in the post
And hear them flop.

Phyllis Dunn

THE LOVELIEST SOUND IN THE WORLD

Some love the sound of church bells ringing
Others, the dawn chorus of birds singing
The soothing sound of waves 'gainst the shore
The sound of music in the evening air

But to me the loveliest sound by far
To which there is no language bar
Today, tomorrow and ever after
Is the sound of children's laughter

The world needs love, and the world needs laughter
Give freely of one and the other follows after
Replace them with greed, anger and fears
And love turns to hate and laughter to tears

There is food enough in the world to spare
If only we had the will to share
The children of Kosovo, hungry and weary
How can they laugh when life is so dreary?

When I die, if my sins are forgiven
And I stand before the Gates of Heaven
My fondest hope in the Great Hereafter
Is to hear the sound of children's laughter.

Jack Webb

GOD'S HAVEN OF THE MIND

Journeying from a world that knows no change
From war and death to God's unchanging height
Where love and life made new and strange
In blessed silence leap to light
I found perfection set in calm delight.
A prodigal, speeding on my homeward way
After the vanished years, thus did I go,
Turning my face away, lest I should stay
And die in staying; so must we grow
Immortal in our quest and in contemplation find
The hills that only God and Angels know,
Beyond our mortal country of the blind
Till our lives are set in truth and grace
And we see the glory of our Saviour's face.

Uvedale Tristram

DAYS TO REMEMBER

A lovely haze of shimmering blue,
With scent of lavender's magnificent hue.
To catch the early morning sun,
A golden-edge cloud following with fun.
The fading rainbow's vibrant glow,
Warning us a shower will show.
Over a stream the willows weep,
Reflections showing in waters deep.
Waves tumbling gaily onto the shore,
Gently kiss the golden sands once more.
Standing upon the sand dunes high,
We watch in mind days gone by.
The days to remember long after we have gone,
Perhaps they will play our favourite song.

Elisabeth Dill Perrin

A VERY SPECIAL LOVE

'Twixt Grandma and her grandchildren
Exists a special bond,
To them she always has the time
To listen and respond.
She's never in a hurry
And always seems to know
Just exactly how to please
With smiling face aglow;
Safe in her gen'rous tender arms,
Dispensing common-sense,
Her wise advice to them when sought
From life's experience.
Her tender hugs betray the love
You know she feels for you
No one could ever take her place,
She's young as springtime too.
Those summer outings - picnics shared,
Sun always seemed to shine,
As long as Grandma's in their lives
The world will be just fine.
At mealtimes she just seems to know
What treats will bring delight
Those lovely stories on her knee
On freezing winter nights.
Beyond the shadow of a doubt
The bond is like no other
The love, the joy, the sweet content,
'Twixt Grandchild and Grandmother.

Peter Fordham

A GARDEN OF PRAISE

Praise and sweetness, a musty smell
A land of virtue, a heart that swells.
A garden full of applause and praise
Milk and honey on which to graze.

Luscious pasturage in meadows grand
The Lord in goodness held out His hand.
And we in turn held ours out too,
Then came the glorious wonderful view.

A garden of praise, a tribute in glory
For all of us could tell a story.
No matter how the Truth we learned
In our heart it does but burn.

Denise Shaw

THE LONER

The Loner: that's what I'll always be.
That's how I was born and how people see me.
I wish every day I could prove it untrue,
And feel myself fit in with them and with you.
I long to feel part of some body or crowd,
To know I belong and to feel myself proud.
From childhood I've searched all in vain for my role,
But even in marriage I still felt alone.
I suppose it's no wonder it all fell apart,
While relief interlaced every ache of my heart.
Oh, just to be normal and not feel this way.
Why can't I stop wanting to hide right away?
Why must I feel good in silence, alone?
So tranquil and happy, complete on my own.
Is it gift or black curse to be so out of pace,
To be quietly fulfilled in my own special space?
To be self-sufficient, yet a misfit as well?
I can't work it out.
Is it heaven, or hell?

Helen McLean

SEA BREAK

Fathoms have taken the hour.
Somewhere in green depths flower
The sea-moments we have known.
Now, like the seagull, we go
Over the day's ebb and flow,
Flying where fancy has flown.

We value the day that slips
To a quiet golden eclipse
Though we've little to count it by.
Yet those moments gone to the sea
Are more dear in our memory
Than all the stars in the sky.

Pamela Constantine

THE ROSE

I've a beautiful Rose in my garden
It is fragrant and fully in bloom
The bees seek for nectar within it
They visit at dawn, dusk and noon.

But whence did that Rose get its beauty
It looked upwards and opened its heart
And the sun shone a warm beam upon it
Creating loveliness right from the start

And the rain played its part in like manner
It gave of itself to that Rose
And its needs were supplied without asking,
That's like trusting the Lord I suppose.

If we open our hearts to the Saviour
He becomes the sun (Son) of our lives
Then the warmth of His love will work wonders
As through life all our *needs* are supplied.

Muriel I Tate

There's No 'Art' In It

I went to an art exhibition displaying the modern kind
Where a yellow brick wall hung with pictures of eggshells and
bacon rind
Banana skins too had been painted - as had apple and orange peel
What the artists were trying to tell us I just wasn't able to feel
Further on was another example of how to project the bizarre
A number of weeds and an orchid were stuck in a dirty jam jar
Self-expression had really run riot - as everywhere strange objects stood
Politicians were modelled in plaster (except the heads which were made
out of wood)
Two large compressed pieces of metal that were once proudly-owned
motor cars
Stood alongside a rocket-powered dustbin - with a notice 'This way
to Mars'
Next a wheelbarrow tied to a tandem - boasted 'energy-saving'
for farms
It may be a saving on fuel - but not much good on the legs and arms
Huge piles of bricks and bundles of sticks were expressions of
someone's delight
While a bag of cement and a shovel was labelled 'Construction Site'
A telephone box painted purple stood alone like some forbidding tomb
A notice displayed on the outside read - 'To let (own phone)
single room'
I marvelled at what other sights I might see - and shortly encountered
more 'skills'
Two rotary blades on a couple of spades were entitled
'Tomorrow's windmills'
And an old kitchen sink was filled to the brink with screwdrivers,
hammers and drills
Though I left unimpressed with the talent - the message came through
loud and clear
I would search in the attic for any old junk - and enter it all next year.

Joan Brown

LUNCHTIME STORY

'Look at this advert' said a friend of mine
to a group of us chatting one lunchtime.
'Draughtsmen required for a large bakery
I think I'll apply, it's a good salary.'
The first man exclaimed, 'It sounds a good job
with plenty of dough for making a cob.'
The second declared 'I don't think I'll try,
for I don't knead it, I'll just pass it by.'
The third man stated 'I'll try it too
you can loaf about, so I'll join the queue.'
The fourth man added 'You can add my name
for I'm currently thinking of joining the game.'
The fifth man shouted 'It's my birthday soon
they are sure to give me a raise in June.'
The sixth man added 'I might have a go,
perhaps buy a Rolls, I'll stand in the row.'
'He won't laugh at that,' said the seventh man
'he can be a crusty devil and seedy so he can.'
The eighth one said 'It may be for me
different flours for the wife to see.'
'Crumbs,' said number nine, 'I'll drink a toast
I'm sure to get it, I don't knead to boast.'
Number ten then said 'Help me for my sake
I'll take a slice, it's a piece of cake.'
'Yes, that's for me' said the number eleven
I was born and bred for it, perhaps in heaven.'
Then someone else asked 'And what about you?
I'm sure you can tell us a joke or two.'
'Well,' I replied, 'I was thinking if I joined
I might get a trip out the yeast' I coined.

Terry Daley

AWAY WE GO!
(Through my children's eyes)

We travel on the motorways,
Yes, we are on our holidays
To set off in the night seems fun
Till maps have to be read by Mum!

She thinks she know what she's about
Then Dad says 'Where is this roundabout?'
Mum fumbles in the dark, we see,
Not a clue has she, where we might be!

'That's it,' cries Dad, 'we'll have to stop,
Shall we have a drink of pop?'
The children say: 'We are so dry'
Dad glares at Mum, oh my, oh my!

Dad sighs, 'We've missed our turning now
You can't map read; I've shown you how!'
Mum sits all quiet, she's boobed once more
It happens every year, we're sure.

Dad starts to fight with maps and things
I think Mum wishes she had wings
Then she could fly to destination
Without the fuss and complication.

Carole O'Neil

THE RHYME AND THE REASON

There's a rhyme and a reason
For everything here on earth,
From the moment of conception
To the day of birth.

The mysteries are endless
We are challenged every day
From the moment of our conception
As we travel on life's way.

The rhyme or the reason
We may never know
From the time of our conception
Till God says it's time to go.

M Lindsey

THE STRAY DOG

I met you one day as I drove into my street.
Your skeletal form made my heart bleat.
Stumbling uncaring, searching for food,
I wondered how you would feed your brood.

You had puppies, I knew, somewhere crying,
Waiting for food, so you keep on trying,
Looking for scraps or anything to eat;
You were gone in a flash before we could meet.

I have never managed to see you again.
Your situation fills me with pain.
I pray you will find someone who will supply your need
In your desperation and give you a feed.

But not only that - help you find a home,
So you never have to always roam,
Looking for the basics that my dogs share -
Food and shelter, love and care.

Patricia Forsberg

ENGLISH PRIDE

English pride was at its highest,
Long ago in forty-five.
The first newsflash was the brightest,
Soon VE Day did arrive.
That was England's finest hour,
At the time of victory,
Over the most evil power,
That could surely ever be.
Many people were deserving
Thanks for all their fortitude.
Soldiers, sailors, airmen, serving,
Played their parts to war conclude.
But, praise God, His intervention
Came with odds against them laid.
On more times than I can mention,
Did He come to England's aid.

English pride was at its lowest,
In two thousand, one bad day,
And the newsflash was the vilest,
Football fans caused much dismay.
Then, instead of English heroes,
Belgian friends to well acclaim,
There were English desperadoes,
Bringing to our nation shame.
May such fellows know obstruction,
To prevent their wickedness
And then seek the Lord's instruction,
So to find how God will bless.

D J Price

BEDU CALL

I've lived in the desert, heard the Sand sing,
seen the quick flash of a hawk on the wing,
I've sat with the Bedu - host and proud guest -
drinking their coffee, cross-legged with the rest.
Afternoon majlis in sheikhly black tent
towering, welcoming, often I went -
their finely-wrought faces, deep fierce brown eyes,
the grunts of the camels, struggling to rise,
kunjas and rifles, kafiyihs, agals,
rice and boiled mutton, dates and shamals.

The fireball of sun, it sets for the night
enflaming the west with brilliant red light -
then comes the spell of the quiet desert moon
silvering the heaven, softening the dune,
bringing to life in one priceless brocade
deep vistas of stars in regal parade.

Edward Fursdon

SEA, LAND, AIR

I cover every single latitude
By being rough and being crude,
I follow every tiny millimetre
By being a top world-beater.
I follow the Tropic of Capricorn
By being the Crown Prince of Porn.
I cover the length of the equator
By being a slob and woman hater.
I stick to each of the ley lines
By smuggling fags and cheap French wine

I measure every single longitude
By being an pig and downright rude
I set sail on every high tide
By being a Jekyll and Mr Hyde
I navigate each mighty ocean
By being a bigot without a notion
I cross the wide Seven Seas
By making girls nice to please.
I sit and watch every bright star
By being allowed to go too far.

Colin Allsop

RAISE ON HIGH

What's there for you
  The same for me
On boughs and roots
  Of every tree,
Where love sublime
  Doth eagerly wait
To open up her golden gate.
  When patience moulds
The clod and star air
  To banish the mist
That holds you there.
  Captive to trait
And wayward scorn,
  'Tis God who renews
Our ways reborn.
  Time tells of vision
As yet may see
  From root to bough
And leaf on tree;
  Hold not the frost
Of summer season,
  Give spirit to space
And melt the reason.

Nick Purchase

VULNERABLE

She looked small, fragile, was alone,
But she hates being on her own.
An affair has again ended,
She wants her broken heart mended.

She knows this will take a long time,
And worries fill her troubled mind.
She's trying hard to carry on,
Difficult now her lover's gone.

When I visited her today,
Her tears never seemed far away.
If any can bear this she can,
Poor vulnerable woman.

S Mullinger

HENRY VIII

Henry the Eighth had six wives
He didn't care about others' lives
When he asked Rome for a divorce
He wanted the reply 'Yes, of course.'

The Pope said 'No. It can't be done.
You're married for life to only one.'
But Henry replied 'I want a change'
So he himself decided to arrange.

To have five more wives and to head
The new church and take to bed
His future spouses in their turn
So the decisions were his concern.

Two wives beheaded as was their fate
They didn't survive their 'Live By' date
So he continued to do his own thing
Proving to all that he was 'The King'.

Michael A Leonard

MY DAY AT THE SEASIDE

What a sunny day and a blue sky . . . my!
How they brighten up my eyes
Gone are my cares and woes
It makes me think of holidays and where I'll go
Should I go to a far-off land?
Basking by the sea, lying on silver sand - or
Should I take a cruise?
On a luxury ship . . . and me dining at the captain's table
Fancy me, in evening gown . . . and it, all trimmed with sable

Dreams, that's all, just dreams . . . ! They're not for me
Lucky am I with a day trip by the sea
Going on a local bus -
With folks I know, they don't make a fuss
Just a singalong as we come home
All I will buy . . . just a stick o' rock, maybe a sugar gnome
What a day we'll have . . . then f'me, it's holidays over
Whilst coming home someone shouts . . . 'Don't forget driver!'
Not bad for my holiday . . . it's cost
About a fiver!

Leslie F Dukes

HANGOVER

In a twilight world
Between night and day
A headache that won't go away
Tongue that tastes
Of dirty socks
Body weighted down with rocks
Morning after
Night before
Feeling fragile ever so sore
Brain dysfunction
Vision blurred
Mouth maligned speech is slurred
You're heading for
A mighty fall
One too many that was all!

Karen Jones

TIME

The clock on the wall ticks on and on,
seconds go by, work to done,
seconds to minutes, wasted, oh my,
minutes to hours, sixty in one,
time now gone,
hours to days, twenty-four to go,
make use, don't waste;
days to weeks, one of seven,
before we know it, here comes heaven:
weeks to months, four I'm told,
months to years growing old,
years fly past, one by one,
use it *time* precious *time*
before it's all gone.

Catherine Torode

I HAVE NO WORDS

You ask me if I write my screed
About religion or my faith.
Am I like venerable Bede
In mists of time, a passing wraith?
I have no words, there is no praise
To extol my glorious Lord.
His creations fill my days
Where nature blooms in full accord,
Far greater poets, writers too,
Their impressions have recorded.
Who am I to say what is true
What is righteous, what is ordered
In heaven's infinite glory?
I know no eulogies, phrases none,
To tell the inspiring story
Of seasons passed away and gone
When our Creator showed his power
And made this Earth beneath my feet
Resplendent in each verdant bower,
With crystal waters cool and sweet.
I am aware he slumbers not,
Nor does that power ever wane
To cleanse this globe, leaving no spot,
(Inheritance from men like Cain
Whose greed has shadowed mankind's home),
But radiant soon it will arise
A shining star in Heaven's dome;
Yet but a stool for God so wise,
Who lovingly permits us still
Around his feet to sit with eyes
Adoring. We live to serve your will!

Evelyn Balmain

THE CURSED CASTLE

A castle stood in days of yore
Upon a rock, beside a shore,
A dismal place, and what is more
A princess lived alone there.

No flower no fern, no leafy wood,
The mists clung closer than they should
Only the seagulls came for food,
From the princess all alone there.

The winds around blew cold and terse
Around its tower there hangs a curse
No mice, no rats and what is worse,
The princess lived alone there.

Until some prince came riding by
Strong of limb and bright of eye,
And harkened to the maiden's cry
The princess had to stay there.

A handsome prince, troops after him,
Came riding past the castle grim,
Thought, there's a place to hide within.
The princess let him stay there.

The castle blossomed overnight
Through every window, filtered light,
The princess dressed herself in white
For marriage to her prince there.

The prince was full of happiness
His princess glowed with loveliness,
The castle sighed with thankfulness
To be no longer cursed there.

And there it stands unto this day
As people pass, you'll hear them say
What joy there lingers in this bay,
And the castle on the rock there.

Dorothy Beaumont

THE POTTERY CLASS

My husband goes to pottery class, every Tuesday morn,
He's going to make a coil pot, the patio to adorn.
He starts to roll the clay, ready for the base,
Then he makes the coils, and puts them into place.
It takes a bit of doing, this shaping by hand,
Now it's nearly finished, it's looking rather grand.
It's time to have a coffee break, and a little chat,
To praise each other's work of art, they talk of this and that.
Then it's back to his creation, he gives his pot a pat,
It's ready now to be fired, he brings it home to view.
Then some bright spark says, is it my eye, or is it a bit askew?
He says he'll try the wheel next time, but I'm not so sure,
The last time he tried it, it ended on the floor.
So he'll stick to making coil pots, when all is said and done,
They all will be his masterpiece, every single one.

Dulcie Beatrice Gillman

IN ITS SHELL

Shell, half-concealed in sand. Inmate living.
It knows that waves must advance, must retreat.
Ever anxious a predator to cheat,
To stay in shallow pools more than willing -
Covered and caressed by tangled seaweed -
Or sliding between multicoloured stones
Or even white fragments of animal bones -
Wherever found, shell-protection at need.
So, how pass such transient hours of peace?
Can it imagine coasts of cream and gold,
An ocean where currents do not run cold?
Where, shell wide open, it lies safe, at ease . . .

Too soon, moon-shifted tides come rolling back.
Time to be certain no shell is left slack.

Chris Creedon

HITTING THE MODEST HIGH SPOTS!

I'm never at a loss, thank God,
for utilising time!
How often in one's married life
does one *have* this joy of mine?
One waits a goodly part of day,
alone or part of two
and out comes pen and what you will
to record the moment's view.
I've written lots and lots of stuff
throughout a life-time long;
there's nothing of eternal worth
nor even *like* a song.
But that which happens all the time
exciting no comment
is worthy of this pen of mine -
with that, I'm quite content

Andrew A Duncan

A TIME FOR RHYME

A blank page stares me in the face,
I must get away from this mundane place,
I take the train to a faraway town,
My face fast losing its weekday frown.

I look out of the window at things
Running past: first I see a poor old thing
Struggling along, weighed down by baggage,
Behind her, a cripple painfully entering a carriage.

Across the fields, a farmer rounding up cattle,
Some going easily, others looking for battle;
Under a hedge a woman feeding a goat,
Her golden hair escaping and flowing about.

A small child having fun on his trike,
Then along come a couple out on a hike,
Their young faces glowing in the brisk air,
Their eyes reflecting beauty and calm everywhere.

What a charming picture to have before me,
Now I can fill the blank page with my story.

Mary Frances Mooney

FREEDOM'S DREAM

Freedom's dream, I'll call her that.
What name more fitting for my yacht?
She'll be sleek and clean of line,
I can see her now through future's time.

    We'll sail off heading west
    Heaving to where I think is best.
    Ports of call and oceans wide
    Heading out on a turning tide

From crest to trough she'll ride the swell
At the helm I'll stand through Heaven and Hell
There are no roots in the mighty sea
No ties or binders when sailing free

    Weathering storms and squalls and sun
    Working on deck for a sip of rum,
    From one landfall until the next
    We'll sail together with no regrets.

Lee Spencer

CONVERSATION PIECE

Please forgive my speculation
but I have an odd sensation
that we once met at this station
almost every day

In a play by Noel Coward
when our brief encounter flowered
into romance my name's Howard
by the way

And unless I'm much mistaken
yours is Johnson And it's taken
all these years to re-awaken
our private lives of yesterday

James Hodgson

A TIME FOR RHYME

I look at the clock to see the time
I sit and watch the minutes tick by
My nerves are so bad I could sit and cry
I go into the dentist he says 'Open wide'
Great relief my teeth are just fine

Gillian Morrisey

RED IS . . .

Red is:-
Postman's van and pillar box,
Little round blobs of chicken pox.

Holly berries and Santa Claus,
Fine red paint upon the doors.

Salvia spikes and geranium,
Large protuberance of bubble gum.

Beach umbrellas and lobsters' claws
Great, wide cavern of a monster's jaws.

Rubies and roses, clowns' red noses,
Red-rimmed eyes and evening skies,
Valentines' hearts and temperature charts,
Traffic lights and dancers' tights,
Balloons and brolly, always jolly,
Red-breasted robins, fishing floats bobbing.

Embarrassed faces flushing and blushing,
Blood from arteries spurting and gushing.

Red-hot pokers and glowing coats,
Hell and damnation for burning souls.

Blobs of jam in small round tarts,
Were they made by the Queen of Hearts?

Scarlet, crimson, carmine, red,
Vermilion, cherry, rosy-red
Red . . .
     Red . . .
          Red.

Marjorie Haddon

AND WE'RE OFF

Onward, onward going with the flow,
Onwards, northwards heading for the snow.
Black shapes, grey shapes, looming from the mist,
Early morn, early dawn, the sun is yet to kiss.
Hampshire, Winchester home of Alf the Great,
Get going, get going or else we shall be late.
To London, then Yorkshire along the roads we pound,
Swaying and swishing along a motorway of sound.

Ray Lewis

THE QUEEN'S VISIT

"So, Michael, where have you been?"
"Well, to see the Queen;
that's what I've been up to today!
She came not very far away -
to our local Civic Hall,
but that's not all.
She spoke with me.
Now, She's a lovely lady.
No airs and graces.
She picked me out of a sea of faces.
In my wheelchair I was sat down.
Now, although I wore no crown
She came over and chatted with me,
even though I have a disability!"
"Good morning Your Majesty
and welcome to Connah's Quay!
Ma'am your son - our future King,
in common we have one thing
and that is Operation Raleigh.
Now, our Prince Charlie; ·
He supported that venture -
a true-life 'Boy's Own' adventure!"

Michael W Williams

ZEPHYR

A lonely wind
Without a home
Born an orphan
Born to roam

A virgin wind
Without a spouse
Born a lion
Born a mouse

A barren wind
Without a child
Born so gentle
Born so wild

A psychotic wind
With moody swings
Untamed by paupers
Untamed by kings

A muted wind
Coming from where
No time for roots
No life to share

An unchained wind
With wanderlust
Stirring the trees
Stirring the dust

So sad a wind
Cursed to move on
Listen to it singing
Its lonely song.

David Watson

WHERE THE WIND BLOWS

Take what you need
Just drift like a dandelion seed
Go where the wind blows
Where you may end, nobody knows
Let go the blossom and drift away
Drift on the spirit of each new day
And if some day you should float away
I'll remember your golden face
Your smile and the things you didn't say.

Clive Cornwall

THE SKY'S LIT UP

The sky darkened the clouds looked angry.
I walked faster along
For I did not want to be caught up in bad weather,
Whatever it be.
The skies opened the lightning flashed
The thunder it roared,
Then down came the rain - it poured
What next, a flash of lightning hit a tree,
I ran fast as the tree was falling towards me.
I made it, and the tree crashed to the ground.
The thunder still putting its noise all around.
Still going along fast as I could go,
The skies were lighting up
Like sheets of cross-fire without a bow.
I saw an old barn - I ran inside in fright,
That evening I felt I would lose my life.
Then the barn roof caught fire, by another flash,
My heart could take no more, I thought I'd not last,
Then I heard a voice say, 'Do not fear,
I am with you always - I am here.'
Then all went still all around
No more thunder, no more lightning came.
Going home I felt easy inside
Knowing my Lord had saved my life.

Marion Staddon

FROM THE PONY TO THE PHONE

Pony Express carrying the mail.
All that will change as
it all turns to rail.
Tracks laid down
From Colorado to Texas.
Men working hard,
Long hours and restless.
Back in the shanty towns,
It's a bath and a beer.
A laugh and a joke,
Perhaps a girl standing close - near.
Maybe the barbers for a shave and a trim.
A long game of cards,
Hoping you win
Some extra cash for the wife
and the kids,
To spend how they like,
As long as they live.
Communication is coming,
By train each new day.
Telegraph poles spotted-out
Wide in array.
Calls coming through
At an alarming rate,
The phone is now here
. . . Make no mistake . . .

Michael John Swain

GIFTS FROM GOD

Sitting in the garden
Midst many lovely flowers.
The air is full of sweetness
From honeysuckle bowers.

Birds are flying here and there
And stop at times to sing.
While silently the butterflies
Flit by on dainty wings.

The scene is one of peace and calm
With nature at her best.
It speaks of One who gave it life
And bids us in Him rest.

A childhood hymn too comes to mind
And helps us to understand.
That large or small each living thing
Was made by His own hand.

Eyes to see and ears to hear
And senses to take in.
These many wondrous gifts from God
Should not we praises sing.
Thank you for the world so sweet
Thank you for the food we eat.
Thank you for the birds that sing
Thank you Lord for everything.

F L Brain

LOVE

Straight, swift, swallows fly
towards the evening sun
golden year is done
gardeners' time is passing by;
through trees, breezes sigh
summer's heart has begun;
life and love merge as one
starlight glitters in the sky
slumbering days soon out-run
sleepy eyes of the sun;
love's romance is never done
let last few roses die
we are lovers you and I
in love's lips my roses lie.

T M Webster

RHYMING SPRING

Many seek the rhyme-a-time
Simple lilt in rhythmic line
Their inspiration to underline
The verities to state, not mime

So have the words we seek so oft'
Flowed and spoke aloft
Where none scoffed
And as the scents of spring waft soft

And weave a time anew
This garden unplanted as we grew
In unpoetic barb and poison too
Now part of the words we strew

And where the bards on nature sang
The ominous page was turned to slang
With cruelty's tang
From the scientific gang

But not too late to poetise
On 'scapes fair and far to humanise
In breathless days for beauteous animals to memorise
And these poems to realise.

John Amsden

GULLS GALORE

Five seagulls flying high
Coming near the shore
One went a paddling
Then there was four.

Four seagulls flying slow
Landing on the sea
One never saw the shark
Then there were three.

Three seagulls flying fast
Past a fishing crew
One got entwined in nets
Then there were two.

Two seagulls flying low
Spied a fair of fun
One went on the dodgem cars
Then there was one.

One seagull on the beach
Singing a lonely song
Befriended by a little girl
Then there were none.

E J Watson

MIRAGE

'You're playing very well tonight,'
The Fiddler told me earlier on.
'Not a single note was out of place,
And the beat, it was spot-on.'

I thought, at last I've done it,
And really played with meaning.
When I woke up with a juddering start,
And realised I'd been dreaming.

'That note was out of tune,' he said,
'Your beat is out of time.'
So *this* is my reality,
Will I ever reach my prime?

Peter Lee

HOARDERS

The shed is full of hoards
Alike a local shopping store
Pots of paint half-filled
Bags of sand torn and split
Old clothes saved for rags
Many sizes of paper bags
Paint brushes gone hard and dry
Pots of nails way up high
Cycle wheels we will never use
Electric gadgets without a fuse
In the house there must be more
Stuffed behind the cupboard door
Old papers with stale news
Worn out dusty shoes
Short and long bits of string
Odd buttons in a tin
Clothes bought so long ago -
Hems were high and knees did show
Items bought for a spare
Then just left sitting there .
I hate throwing things away
They will be used one day.

Sheila Waller

EUROVISION

Exchange of culture
In music and words
A melody of tongues
From Europe's nations
In a musical celebration
Of talent and admiration
Most of us realise
The need to culturise
Love it or loathe
It's there you know
Celebrate our customs and styles
For a while
In collaboration
With other nations
Then you see
Hands across the sea

P Edwards

THE CAUTIONARY TALE OF FREDDIE PHIPPS

(A moral tale of winter mourning;
He heeded not the weather warning.)

The chief delight of Freddie Phipps
Was going off on country trips.
He'd fill a flask and pack his lunch,
And take a choc'late bar to munch.
He'd do the car things which he ought ta'
Like check the tyres and fuel and water.
He'd say 'Poop, poop' like Mister Toad
And head out on the open road.

One morning on the radio
It said 'We think it's going to snow,'
But this did not deter our Freddie,
'I'm going to go since I am ready.'
And when in time the sky turned black,
'I've come so far, I'll not turn back.'

The wind came up and the snow came down.
Our Freddie then began to frown.
The wind it blew and the snow it snew
And quite obscured the forward view.
It was, I hear, a week or more
Before they found him in the thaw.

Enjoy yourselves, have lots of fun.
But always travel in the sun.
Be careful when it rains or hails,
Avoid the lightning and the gales.
And children, friends, be warned by me
That when you hear the BBC
Say that it is going to snow,
You must never, never go.

Mike

THE YEAR IN VERSE

January can be bleak and cold,
February evermore so bold,
In March the weather starts to turn,
Winter, April starts to spurn,
In May, spring flowers all come out,
June, summer's influence is all about,
July, the children break up from school,
Sweltering August, it's hard to keep cool,
In September the tones of autumn are near,
October has skies so blue and so clear,
November has frosts and Guy Fawkes night,
December with Christmas and snow so white,
The seasons change as the months go by,
What colours and wonders grace the eye.

Christine Nolan

MY MOTHER-IN-LAW

She goes to church nearly every day,
She always has time to hear what you say,
She helps all she can, if only in prayer,
She walks many miles to give comfort and cheer,
And everyone is happier when she is near,
I for one think she's a perfect dear,
For she's my mother-in-law,
When she visits the needy she has something to take,
Either flowers or books or she bakes a cake,
But she's not rich she's a pensioner like you,
That's why she walks, to save a copper or two,
She gets such happiness by giving to others,
But she's as dear to me as my own mother.

Jan Graver-Wild

ECOLOGICALLY SOUND

I wish I'd cleared up in the autumn
When the weather was sunny and mild,
For you know what they say,
If you idle today,
Tomorrow it's bound to be wild!

My garden's a small creature's haven
And it did seem a little unkind
To cut all the stems
Of the plants to the hems -
So I left all the rubbish behind.

I wanted leaf litter for hedgehogs
To go into snug hibernation,
And dry, twiggy bowers
Around all the flowers
To protect little moths in pupation.

Every shrub is well-covered in seed heads.
I must say, they have run a bit rife,
But each tiny seed
Is fulfilling a need
And it may save a starving bird's life.

But there's so much to do in the garden,
Winter rain is beginning to pour,
So I'm moved to confess,
Contemplating the mess,
That I wish I had cleared up before!

Jean Oxley

HOT AIR BALLOONS

Must we get out the dictionary book
pedantic rubbish can't overlook
Keep it simple, write it plain
hidden meaning supposed to explain

He she or it is - what's the trick
put pen to paper, the clever dick
Long drawn-out mind games
for the intellectual twit

Give me Kipling with his 'If'
a lasting masterpiece of ad lib
Straight from the heart
for all to understand

Than the garbage and dribble
of the matter in hand
Complicated thought from a complicated mind
enough of that in life to find

To read it in poetic form
afraid for me it's just too strong
Rhyming verse better by far
the latter prose already a blur

Say what you mean, understand the play
perhaps that sounds a bit au fait
Liken to a will, all gobbledegook
be as well with the dictionary book . . .

Jean Tennent Mitchell

OLD YELLOW

When I was small, only about seven,
I think I received a gift from heaven.
A man came tapping upon our door,
To say Mrs Watson was no more.
A dear old lady from down the lane,
So kind and gentle, like tender rain.

Within his arms, he held a dog,
Who was found a-roaming in the fog.
Just a puppy, that poor soul to see,
Mrs Watson left him, just for me.
I cried with joy, and called him Yellow,
Because his nature, was so mellow.

As I grew up, and became a man,
Old Yellow was a faithful fan.
We loved each other, like nothing heard,
For him I always prayed a word.
Faithful, loyal, to everyone around,
For Yellow, I turned down one thousand pound.

One day along the river bank I walked,
With old Yellow I talked and talked.
Until, we heard a deafening scream,
Some soul had fallen into the stream,
Old Yellow dived in and swam out there,
And brought them safe, without a care.

Suddenly, old Yellow had disappeared,
Don't say he's drowned, that's what I feared.
No trace of him was ever found,
He must have been taken unto heavenly ground.
He saved a life, at the cost of his own.
Old Yellow, no faith so great was known.

Steve Kettlewell

PATIENCE IS A VIRTUE!

As I was driving one day into town
The woman in front of me was making me frown
She was driving far too slow
So on the horn I was ready to blow!

I cursed and swore and drummed my fingers
But no shifting the woman, she continued to linger
Until I turned off at another street
I stamped in frustration and hurt my feet!

Down the town was quiet and quick
Back to the car lickety-split
But on the road home, I wondered why
I was rattling my fingers whilst trying to drive?

I looked at the car in front of me
Oh Lord, I did not want to believe
It was that same woman from earlier on
Going home on her journey, I laughed not frowned!

As I laughed, I thought of the Lord
And how *He* was chuckling in heaven out loud
'Alright!' I wailed, 'I repent of my sins'
I've learnt my lesson, be patient within!

Diane Simpson

ETHICS

The principles which govern human acts,
(And moral obligation brings to bear),
Are not the same as consequential Law
But life-long truths, distilled from salient facts,
To furnish ethics, purified and clear.
Of these consensus pays respect to four.
'Beneficence', (the art of 'doing good
To others', if we know but who they are),
Derives from whom its virtue falls upon.
Its counterpart, (now widely understood
To be 'avoiding harm to folk'), is far
The safest ethic, also known as 'Non-
Maleficence', (a dark, unwieldy term).
Of self-determination much is made,
('Autonomy', the foremost of the three),
Not absolute, but that it stands the firm
Foundation of whatever else is said
In ethics, even altruists agree.
Then, fourthly, 'Justice', equal law for all,
That innate sense of fairness, widely met,
Whereby each scarce resource is duly shared.
These four, the voice of conscience, sound their call
Across the years that we may not forget
The truths for which all honest minds have cared.

John M Beazley

ONE ANOTHER

In spectrumed light I see the truth
Truth that belongs to us alone.
And harmony plays softer hues
Within our oneness fine in tone;

Believe me for my subtler love
Do not my lesser self become
Stay all alone, stay always near
Your heart will thus become my home.

To touch within the flesh the soul
Is gain: is to be free, not bound;
In secret we will share our love
And celebrate what has been found.

John Rae Walker

THE GO-BETWEEN

Let's put the past behind us
And start afresh today
Memories we all have
No one can take them away
Little things we have said
From within our own heads
Stop and think and change it please
Talk to each other let the pain ease
I know it will be hard to make the first move
Pick up the phone and put finger into the groove
Life's too short, time is passing us by
Start today, please do try
Let it come straight from the heart
Let bygones be bygones don't keep us apart
I miss the company of family and friends too
Please make an effort and make my wish come true

Janice Nice

WOBBLER

Some people get angry
Others rave and rant
Some throw complete wobblers
Then launch things like cutlery and plants
There are a small minority
Who nameless shall remain
No matter what the consequences
They always stay the same

We should envy this talent
For staying on the track
Take a leaf from their book
Delegate the stress
Then you too can be laid back

C J Collins-Reed

JANUARY

January's plate is bleak and thin -
Much too slim to fill the skin;
With berries near gone and shoots too tight,
Cold by day and colder the night,
Shiver and search then shiver and scratch,
Yet findings for hunger never the match:
Survival is all of each day's intent -
January's life is harshly meant!

John M Reeve

THE HAIRDRESSER'S LAMENT

There's a dolly with a trolley, as cute as can be.
What secrets she hides is a mystery to me.
She rattles away and no one's quite sure -
If it's her bones, or an uneven floor!

No one can see trolley, it's hidden from view
There's curlers all sizes I know this is true.
Paper for perms, cotton wool and yes pins
The tints are secret, under combs and things.

Our dolly has an aura, sweet and demure
Always a smile and will listen to you.
One thing's for sure our dolly is not -
And this of course is, a tart with a cart!

I hope I won't lose my dolly with trolley
It's my only hour off, I'm always so busy.
So Terry keep smiling and pushing your cart
I can't wait to see your next work of art!

Freda Symonds

LIFE'S MUSIC

It isn't just trumpets, piano, or drums,
Accordion, flute or the strings,
Take the hum of bees, the birds in the trees,
We make music on so many things.

As people make music, so oft not aware,
Vibrations can alter all round.
Changing the mood, or the energy flow . . .
Each soul will reflect every sound.

Your voice is an instrument . . . special to you,
To speak, or to sing, or recite.
Telephonist - teacher - or drama on stage,
Good training will bring you delight.

Know as you travel through life's ebb and flow,
Music you're making wherever you go.
The music of life is a thing you should share
Unconditional love shows you *really do* 'care'.

M Gibson

OLIVIA'S RONDEAU

At two weeks old, at my behest,
my grandad holds me on his chest.
Relaxing in his gentle arms
I feel he saves me from alarms.
I sleep and know that it is best
to snuggle in this loving nest.
He'd recognised I need my rest -
at two weeks old.

When I grow up - on my request -
he'll be a very welcome guest.
I'll put my baby in his arms.
He'll save my infant from all harms.
My child will nestle on his breast -
at two weeks old.

Evelyn Golding

THAT CAT

She sits there in a little ball
In contentment and sheer peace,
Her eyelids hardly make a move,
her fur is soft as fleece.
Beside the fire she sits and waits
Until it's time for tea
And strokes her owners heel with love,
She couldn't feel more free!
I love the cat with all my heart,
And would love to be like her:
a soft, warm body day and night,
But just a gentle purr.
I think God made her Queen of Hearts
to be where she is now,
I look on her and feel so glad
To hear that short miaow!

Sharon Howells

JIMMY SMITH

Jimmy Smith had cleared his desk and put his things away
But this time it was different; it was retirement day!
He mustn't be down-hearted, this was not a time for tears;
His friends had fixed a party up to mark his thirty years.

The card was signed by everyone; his present was just great!
His back was slapped so often that he nearly dropped his plate.
With kissing all the ladies and the handshakes everywhere
And all the lengthy speeches there was hardly time to spare.

'You'll certainly be sadly missed; you're irreplaceable,
But have a good retirement and enjoy it to the full.
And don't forget to keep in touch and pop in when you can.
We'll all be glad to see you as you're such a lovely man.'

When, finally, the last 'goodbyes' were said by one and all
He sensed his popularity had made him ten feet tall.
He felt a little tipsy with that extra glass of wine,
But hurried home elated as his 'send off' had been fine.

A month passed by and Jimmy thought he'd like to see his friends
To catch up on the gossip and the little odds and ends.
He walked into reception and was greeted with a smile.
'I'll ring the office manager; just wait a little while.'

The manager received the call and said, 'Right; send him in.'
And then addressed the office staff, announcing with a grin,
'Reception says that Jimmy Smith's about to come on through.'
Their furrowed brows were followed by the question, 'Jimmy *who?*'

Dennis Turner

SPRING TIDE

The sea spray savages the shore
  In dreams,
      And shrouds the memory,
And words of adoration pour
  Like streams,
      Exulting with the sea.

Exulting with the sun-kissed sea,
  They yearn
      For blue and amber days,
When flaxen beauty carolled free
  To turn
      Ingratitude to praise.

To turn ingratitude to praise!
  I know
      My vibrant heart was there
To glean the wonder of her ways,
  And sow
      Its glories everywhere.

S H Smith

TOTAL ECLIPSE

It was the eleventh of August
In nineteen-ninety-nine;
The sun arose, not knowing
What would happen in due time.

As crowds of people gathered
In England's far south west,
They hoped to see a great event
With weather at its best.

That morning, though, was cloudy;
Just a few breaks there, some here.
Then, as the sun shone through them,
The people gave a cheer.

It died away to silence,
As though they were struck dumb,
For there was something missing:
A portion of the sun.

This portion grew much bigger,
Till all the sun was dark;
And nightingale was so confused,
It sang duets with lark.

Then came the diamond ring effect,
As people watched in awe;
It was sublimely beautiful,
They'd not seen it before.

The sun, of course, in time returned;
They saw it through the haze.
The weather, too, was normal -
It rained the next three days.

Roger Williams

Pen And Paper

The pen aligns itself beside the sheet
Of velum snow, its vestal innocence
Untouched by any prints as it would meet
The eye, its face nascent as you commence
Inscribing with the nib which copperplates
Across a width, each letter paraphrases
An idea which emerges and relates
To thought, the mind's own idealistic phases.

And so you pick the pen into your hand,
Training its point onto the maidenhead .
Of that one sheet, and then as thoughts run planned
Into the mind, you pierce until its bled
Its innocence away, how great a bliss
Lies there within a page, the pen would kiss.

A Hopkins

THE MYRTLE TREE

It was just a little Myrtle tree,
Standing in the sand,
Waiting for planting by two firm friends,
Working hand in hand.

Just a little Myrtle tree,
It's flower of purple hue,
Waiting to make memories,
To share between me and you.

Our pretty little Myrtle tree,
Which you can see each day,
That I keep in my mind's eye,
Even when I'm far away.

So treat our little Myrtle tree,
With tender loving care,
And if you ever want to see me,
Look behind it, I'll be there.

P A Kelly

STILL BE FUN

As we get older through the years,
We think of all the happiness and fears.
How as children for hours we did play,
In the fields, amongst the hay.
Staying out till it got dark,
Listening to the nightingale and lark.
Saving to go on a holiday,
By the sea we used to stay.
Having scones with cream and jam,
A salad with pilchards or ham.
Sometimes we'd get a nice treat,
Strawberries, ice-cream or something sweet.
Now our pennies don't go so far,
We still save a few in a jar.
Nor go to the seaside to stay,
We can only walk round a field of hay,
And we can still enjoy the sun,
Sitting at home can still be fun.

Margaret Upson

WHO WILL?

Who will feed the hungry,
Or clothe the naked poor?
Heal the sick and needy
And never shut the door.

Who will offer succour
To stay the hand of need?
Or proffer warmth and comfort;
Who will care to heed?

Who will tender shelter
To escape the heat and cold?
Or sacrifice a luxury,
Who would be so bold?

Who will shield the lowly
From the aggressor's might?
Secure hope from oppression,
Protect them from the fight.

Who will speak for conscience,
Supporting right from wrong?
Showing the light of freedom
To those who don't belong.

Now the day is closing,
Time isn't standing still,
Certain in the knowledge
That if we don't do it . . . Who will?

Bryan Colman Bird

THE WAY TO HEAVEN

Awakening, I feel so well,
My thoughts are calm and clear,
In contrast to my constant hell,
Of agony and fear,
I wonder how I woke up here,
I went to sleep in bed,
To say the least it's very queer,
That I am here instead,
Quite suddenly I am aware,
That I can stand alone,
No walking frame, no mobile chair,
My need for them has gone,
Small groups of people stand around,
With solemn downward stare,
They look as frozen as the ground,
Their breath hangs on the air,
I try to make my presence clear,
But they're ignoring me,
They all have ears that cannot hear,
And eyes that cannot see,
But then I see the grave that's there,
And hear a prayer said,
My name is featured in the prayer,
Which means I must be dead,
I'm sure God knows that I've passed on,
I hope I've been forgiven,
I'll knock upon the nearest stone,
And ask the way to Heaven.

Matthew L Burns

OCTOBER EVENING

The sky glowed red way down in the west
As the day fast drew to its close;
The gentle flowers nodded their petals in sleep.
Slowly, the golden moon rose.

A peace descended o'er the darkening earth,
The nightingale awakened the owl;
The badger nosed drowsily out from his set
To begin his nocturnal prowl.

Home from the fields the old farmer plodded,
Back bent from long hours of toil.
Nose twitching, tail bobbing, the small rabbit ran
'Cross the furrowed autumn soil.

Shadows lengthened as the moon waxed high;
A soft breeze kept the grey mist at bay.
Like miniature lamps the stars winked above;
'Twas the end to a perfect day.

A R Earl

ON GUARD

My Master leaves me every day
to guard his house and home,
So read the notice on the gate
and leave the lock alone.

Don't be fooled for a minute
by my fiercely waving tail.
My teeth are long and sharp
and are never known to fail.

So don't come through the gate
unless you are a friend,
Then, I'll gladly lick your face
and wag my other end.

J Brown

THE CASTLE RUINS

I sit alone in ponderous thought
Of long ago with battles fought.
A Knight, A Baron, each hold a lance,
Their trusty steeds they rear and prance.

The jousting now is soon begun,
'Till battle to the death is won.
As thundering hooves sound in their ears,
The crowd roars out with mighty cheers.

With a fatal blow the victor's found,
As one lies dying on the ground.
These bloody thoughts I'll hold at bay,
And return to pleasures of today.

The castle ruins now at peace,
The beauty of the place won't cease.
Beneath it's ramparts all serene,
A river flows it's quite a scene!

Just through the arches on my right,
A boat floats silently into sight.
With on my left, a thousand trees,
Leaves swaying gently in the breeze.

If only folk would stop and stare,
This wondrous scene is theirs to share.
My heartfelt wish is true and deep,
The peace it brings is mine to keep.

P M Glennon

'YOU, LORD ARE ALL I HAVE,
and you give me all I need'
Psalm 16:5 (GNB)

When friendship fails
And no one cares
That sorrow crushes me,
Think of the nails:
There's One who shares
The pain and agony.

Why look elsewhere
To find the love
That only he can give?
In deep despair,
Just glance above -
Look up at him and live.

A warm embrace,
A loving touch -
When these things are denied,
By God's own grace
I have so much
And in his peace abide.

Why comfort seek
From one who'll fall?
A loved one though he be.
When I am weak,
I can do all
Through Christ who strengthens me.

He's all I have,
This precious Friend.
His is the voice I heed.
Whate'er I crave,
I can depend
On him to meet my need.

Beryl Adamsbaum

GRANNIES' WISDOM

Well, what a surprise - *Experts* just discover
That children can suffer without their mother.
We've been telling them this for many a year
But were told 'You talk nonsense - sorry my dear.
You're only a grandmother, what do *you* know
With ideas old-fashioned - it's really not so.'
We then looked on aghast as crime rates rose high
'Cause kids were all key-latched with no one nearby
And families broke up when mother earned more
Than father the breadwinner, in days of yore.
His pride was stripped from him so he couldn't cope
And felt devastated without any hope.
The children ran wild as they hadn't the love
Or guidance or discipline sought from above.
For with mum out at work and dad far away
They played truant from school and wreaked havoc each day.
Now these *experts* at last have just seen the light -
Tell mums 'Stay at home, put an end to this blight.'
We old-fashioned grannies were right all the time -
Our ideas were never so far out of line.

Paddy Jupp

NIGHT OF THE STORM

I heard his shrill neighing as Pegasus galloped
Without any rider across the night sky,
Through thunder and storm flew this steed of the mighty,
And bright was the burning of zeal in each eye;
A spirit of youth fed his eager endeavour,
Who scattered Earth's floods as he wildly thrashed by!

Strong gales from the west saw him high in the heavens,
Like lightning he streaked as a luminous bolt,
Whilst snorting with joy at his moment of freedom
When whistled wide wings for a sweep of revolt;
Empyrean tracts now surrendered before him,
Nor was there a power to cause him to halt!

'Pegasus . . . Pegasus . . . !' The welkin would echo,
A welkin bemused by this runaway sire,
Far stars, in bewilderment, blinked as he journeyed
Alike to the tumult - not seeming to tire;
Equestrian beauty perfected in movement,
Neck arched in defiance and filled with desire!

Again and again came the flash of his plummet
From deep in the firmament's glorious array,
A comet-like entry from northward to southward,
When Thor's royal rumble acclaimed such display;
These hills gaily glittered with rays as of Summer
Before he had turned and was off and away!

While shrieked the wild winds, so his mimicking answer,
The moon hid away from those hooves of delight,
From furthermost space sped that stallion, unhindered,
Until Bellerophon took charge of the night;
Who, mounting at speed over gates of the morning,
Bade dawn fill the sky with adventurous light . . .
Its hours long warmed by the surge of that flight.

R Gaveston-Knight
The Warwickshire Poet

JUST ONE QUESTION

I wonder why the mean of mind
Look down with scorn on lesser kind
Who tend to like their nets of lace
And proper form in every place,
Whose writing paper must be lined,
Whose verse must rhyme. Oh, what a bind!
It's easier, far, to be unkind.
Just let your feelings flow apace
I wonder why?

Their writing cannot be confined
By rules of metre, form, or blind
Adherence to the laws of case
Or tense or shape. No, that's just base.
Formal style is undermined.
I wonder why?

Frank Henry

WHATEVER THE HOUR

Whatever the hour I'll be missing you
Each and every second that is all that I do
The rain on the window spells out your name
The clock chimes out memories again and again
The night falls lonely and I miss you much more
The day brings false hope as each one before
Stars twinkle and remind me only of love
Clouds create visions in the Heavens above
I'm lost without you here at my side
When you left my heart shrivelled and finally died
Leaving a space where love used to grow
Creating only tears that constantly flow
Whatever the hour the pain gains control
Killing my heart and killing my soul
The pictures you left cause a commotion
Creating rivers of eternal emotion
Whatever the hour, whatever the time
My heart always praying for you to be mine
The hot water runs cold, the days never end
The pain increases so my heart cannot mend
Each second is spent with you on my mind
Open up my heart you are all that you find
Whatever the hour my world's always blue
Whatever the hour I'm thinking of you.

Kim Darwell

CHILD OF MINE

Oh that there were any other way
To see you grow
Then by your tears!
The aspen that would be a tree
Must endure the weathering of years.

And so with you, oh child of mine
Though your own grief
Should cause me pain.
I know the earth can yield no fruit
Without the suffering of beating rain.

Christine Dennison

WELCOME HOME (MY BABY BOY)

My heart has weighed heavy over the years - my guilt,
the route of all of my fears
For when I gave birth to a bonny baby boy - I thought
I was set on a journey of joy
Little did I know happiness was not going to last - that soon
all of my hopes would be dreams of the past
Mum offered to help as mums always do - her intentions were good,
but if she only knew
The heartache I suffered, the buckets I cried - of course
when she asked I always lied
When she took you away you were no more than three -
said it was best, gave you security
A family unit in which to grow - for what my future would hold
nobody could know
And although I saw you almost every day - the role of Mum
I was forbidden to play

The years passed quickly from infant to teens - and the visits
each day because weeks, then months, so it seems
You had new friends and mums were a bore - so I'd wait
on street corners, arrange holidays galore
I spent many nights just wondering if you knew the truth -
how much I wished you were under my roof
Your room I would decorate in case you should call - I had to believe,
it might sound foolish an all
To this day I regret not continuing to fight - but as they all say,
Mum's always right

Now you have grown, almost six feet - I want you to know
I never gave up hope, couldn't admit to defeat
So imagine my joy when I picked up the phone - and heard your sweet
voice saying 'I'm coming home!'
For now when you hug me and wish me goodnight - it no longer
matters if they tug and they fight

Cos despite all the hurt, the sorrow, the pain that's gone on - they can't break the bond between mother and son.

Welcome home, my baby boy!

All my love

Mum

X X X X

Lynne Gaskell

TIME TO RHYME

I seem to've somehow found the time
To write to you . . . The pleasure's mine!
So nice to know you favour rhyme.
For me, these poems are sublime!
For prose I find's a touch malign
And oft I fail to quite define
The meaning of the works design,
Without the metre or the rhyme!
Words are easier to align
Within the passages of time;
And words with rhyme, can soon entwine
To form a meaning to outshine,
They easy aid the mind, enshrine
And store it for a future time
For use with aptitude divine
Reveal a truth to underline!
So you see, I now consign,
All praise to those who love to rhyme;
And long may thoughts and pen, combine
Thus providing time for rhyme.

Patricia Woodley

GARDENER-IN-WAITING

I'm waiting for snowdrops to open,
To tell us that springtime is near.
I'll get out my spade and my trowel
And plan out my gardener's year.

I'm waiting for tulips to open
In rich oriental display.
More colourful even than rainbows
I look for their blooming in May.

I'm waiting for roses to open
Scent and colour in perfect atune.
The queen of our gardens in summer,
The crown of our hoping in June.

I'm waiting for lilies to open,
They should be in bloom in July.
So perfect in grace and in perfume
They'll captivate those who pass by.

A dear friend, but who shall be nameless,
Said 'Gardening's always the same.
You dig and you sow and you struggle
For the weather to put you to shame.'

Dear friend, I can only remember,
In respect of the matter discussed,
How I said, 'You can stick to your housework -
It's always the same old dust!'

So I'm waiting from season to season
And doubtless I'll wait till the end.
Would even a garden in Heaven
Succeed in convincing my friend?

Kathleen M Hatton

THE CHANGING SEASONS

Springs sacred birth
    Of a fresh new dawn
To a suckling mother
    A child is born;
The first tentative steps
    Of a struggling fawn
As he staggers to his feet.

Summer brings
    Her early morning sun;
The dew hangs
    From a web a spider's spun;
She gives youth to the life
    That spring has sprung
And the thirst for knowledge we seek.

Autumn breathes
    Her slow laboured breath;
Her fallen leaves,
    The only life that's left,
Before winter lays
    Her white coat of death;
The land sits lonely and bleak.

Winter sings
    Her lone evening song;
Her cold night
    Hang bitter and long;
Summers morning
    Glow sadly gone,
Waiting for spring's sweet voice to speak.

Marc Tyler

MY BEST FRIEND (BUDDY)

He's my best friend, he's my Buddy
And he loves to head a ball.
We go everywhere together
He's the greatest friend of all.

When we go to the seaside
He loves swimming in the sea.
He likes hot-dogs and ice-cream
All the things I like, you see.

When we go home, I sit in a chair
But he lies on the floor
Yes, you've guessed it, he's my Buddy
My Golden Labrador.

Mary Traynor

FINALE

Every vision
Must end soon,
Barren fields
At last bloom.
Unseeing eyes
Will know light,
All the meek
Will know might.
All must lose
What they gain,
Every tear
Fall in vain.
Unjustly vanquished
Soon will win,
Every sinner
Know their sin.
All confined
Will be free,
Fleeting hours
Eternity.

Gerald Whitehouse

NATURE'S WONDERS

A squirrel ran among the trees
Anticipating winter freeze
Then up the branch he quickly ran
Gathering fir cones he began
He bit off one and ran down fast
But this was not to be the last
For very shortly he came back
Along exactly the same track
Then with great speed he took one more
Thus adding to his winter store ·
Intent on getting a big stock
He worked from one till four o'clock
But who told him winter was near?
But that he knew became quite clear
Sure enough just two days later
Frost came . . . so he knew how to cater
They have no money or warm home
In search of food and drink they roam
To stay alive most do succeed
Nature provides their every need.

Wendy Dedicott

FULL MOON

The moon was full I saw the seas
Through the black wiry trees
The moon was full revealing the mare
On a winter morn lunar cold and bare

The moon was full bright and clear
Orb through the trees shining lear
The moon was full vivacious beaming globe
Through binoculars glare and probe

Etched out like a world atlas
Round ball grey and white mass
The moon was full on a February morn
Sky lit up for to adorn

Majestic power she does impose
The earth below shivered and froze
The moon was full but she had to leave
Amidst cirrus clouds winding weave

Ann Copland

POST CHRISTMAS LUNCH

The rueful remains of the turkey,
The saddening state of the sprouts;
Congealing puddles of gravy,
And of the stuffing
I'm having great doubts.

That glutinous mass of cranberries
Will survive in the fridge
Due to port;
But the ruins of rich Christmas pudding
To the birds I will have to resort.

The bottles of wine are all empty
And everyone's got a high flush.
They're laying around on the carpet
Like digesting snakes in the bush.

But; boiled ham, vol-au-vents
And a cheesecake,
A huge sherry trifle and such,
Lie alongside a great plumloaf;
And the cheese, bread, and chutney are Dutch!

Mince pies, garlic sausage and salad
Reside in the pantry until,
Three hours have passed
And it's tea-time.
Then we're all in again
For The Kill!

Chris Dent

RHYME

Some beautiful poems are written without rhyme,
But very few stand the test of time.
Contemporary verse cannot paint a picture that is really true.
A thing all would-be poets long to do.

'Tis true it's fun delving into the past,
And clever seekin' out how the dye is cast.
But the novelty soon wears thin,
And so once again the old masters are let in.

It is funny when you hear people say,
'Oh I wish we could return to the good old day.
When the words really depicted what the title said,
And at least you weren't left scratching your head.'

When I have seen some of the prize-winning verse,
I thank my lucky stars that I'd chosen to nurse.
One learns a great deal meeting different folk,
And it helps one to see many a joke.

A proper poem can tell a short story,
Only a very few words can emulate glory.
But I'm afraid I've been mystified at times
When I've read just one word and that's supposed to be a line.

Betty Green

BRITISH WEATHER

Many countries enjoy climate,
But we have only weather.
At home then our most pleasant spells
Will just occur whenever.

June so often disappoints,
September cold and wet.
Today the midst of winter
Might be our safest bet.

Our best can crop up anytime, ·
Which can be far from good.
We'd much prefer our better spells
To blossom when they should.

At least we have variety
Keeping interest alive,
For hope is a necessity;
Without it we can't thrive.

So, when we get those perfect days
That give our souls a lift,
We learn the value of surprise
Which makes the perfect gift.

Don Bishop

'OOR RABBIE'

He was born one day in January
In a month that's really cold,
And Scottish folk, all adore him,
From very young to really old.

He was awfy fond, o' the lassies,
A 'bit of a lad', so they say,
But still he was'na' any worse,
Than some young lads, living today.

At least he never tried to deny them,
Cos he mentioned them a' by name.
By making up poems aboot them,
That have now brought him world fame.

He'd never heard o' family planning,
When a' the lassies he would court.
So he'd be working lots of overtime today,
To pay them all 'child-support'.

Jean Hendrie

WE WANT TO BE ALONE . . . OR . . . THE GENERATION GAP

Oh Mum, you know that Roy's coming in tonight,
You said last week, today would be alright.
That's right! He's coming round at seven,
He'll have to leave again about eleven.
We'll play some tapes or watch TV,
I don't know what he'd like to see.
Don't make a fuss - please play it cool,
And don't shake hands - I'd feel a fool -
It's just not done these days.
I know we have some funny ways.
But times are changing . . . Yes!
You'll be just fine in that blue dress.
When you and dad go out, please slip away
In quite a normal, casual way.
Don't act all coy
In front of Roy.
Oh mum, of course we'll be alright,
He isn't staying overnight.
Don't worry - there's a pet,
We've hardly kissed each other . . . Yet!

Stephen R Ramsden

THE COMING OF SPRING

The hardy beech and sturdy oak
Stand frozen 'neath deep winter's cloak,
Their branches white with frosty gleam
Whilst in their sleeping hearts they dream
Of how the stream which laughs and plays
Around their feet on summer days
Plays such a bright and merry tune
On drowsy, carefree afternoons.
They sense the world begin to thaw
And wait with patience for the signs
Of new life, bringing warmer times
To dwellers of the forest floor;
And they bow as the first birds sing
To herald in the coming spring.

Carl Swallow

THE SPIDER

I watched a spider spinning a web,
Such an intricate pattern, like woven thread.
A thing of beauty to behold,
But I was not fooled by this spider bold.
I knew full well that at its conclusion,
Some unwary insect in utter confusion.
Into this pretty trap would fly,
And thus I sadly gave a sigh,
For the fate of the insect,
Who would have to die.

M Wakefield

SPRING

High-soaring hawks made fluffy chicks scurry;
Swifts, and swift swallows, swooped high in blue skies;
Smooth-skinned green frogs croaked, with bright jewelled eyes;
Warty toads waddled, and could not hurry!

Foxes at night, their distant calls eerie;
New born calves, uttering thin, plaintive cries;
Baby lambs butting between mothers' thighs;
White-bibbed black puss, all friendly and purry.

My soul is stained with some shameful things. Still
My heart for infancy's innocence yearns;
When I lie wakeful in my bed at nights
Memory recalls those departed sweet springs, till
Peace fills my soul. And then, balm-like, returns
Seasons of Childhood and Infant Delights!

Dan Pugh

GREENER GRASS

A sleeping dragon, dormant lies
Beneath a magic spell,
For this is the land of make-believe,
With an age-old wishing well.
To reach this land, just close your eyes
Now picture what you will.
A castle drawbridge raised up high
Where time has just stood still.
Maybe *a sleeping princess,*
A *knight* who guards the way.
Who wields a sword so mighty
For the dragon he must slay.
Release the chains and enter,
Remember what you seek
Breathe in the *air of magic,*
Think hard before you speak.
Look down the well, a fervent wish
Beware the dragon's flame.
Should hopes and dreams be granted,
Life will never be the same!

T G Bloodworth

CO-DOT-E-DOT

When you're not into computers
Because you were born too long ago
You tend to get sick of hearing
Co-Dot-E-Dot, W.W.W. Oh.

It's all a lot of nonsense
To people like me
But there they are - all those numbers
In the papers and on TV.
I could have computer training
But I don't fancy surfing the Net
And now that I'm nearing eighty
I don't want that mouse for a pet
So when I see them on the telly
I groan and say 'Oh, no!'
Because I'm sick to death of hearing
Co-Dot, E-Dot, W.W. Oh.

Joan Gilchrist

MIDNIGHT WITH MAN'S BEST FRIEND

The lights are out - they've all gone to bed
At last there is silence in my head.
I can think - I can drink
To my hearts content
When finally off to bed . . . the children are sent!
Just the fridge humming the clock gently ticking
But hold on - a pair of eyes on the floor are still flicking!
I cannot ignore her, or pretend she's not there
Cos she's one of the family, it wouldn't be fair.
Even when she's curled up tight in a ball
She's company for me - no trouble at all
I think she's asleep now
But her ears stand to attention
Cos she's a good security guard
I forgot to mention!

Julie Powell

MAGIC MOMENTS

Look for the magic in your life,
Don't be overcome by toil and strife,
Magic moments when they happen to you,
Often come right out of the blue,
And they are sometimes quite effective,
At putting things in perspective.

A Cooper

THE EYESORE

A previous owner of my house
was terrified of greedy rats
that got in through a garden fence
disturbing all his precious cats.

He built a very solid wall
with tons of mortar holding it,
that made it look so hideous,
(and yet he didn't mind a bit)!

It's such an eyesore though today
I'll have to dress, caress it up,
replace surrounding concrete blocks
with soil to give a great make-up.

I've looked in different catalogues
but find it very hard to choose
the perfect plants to hide this wall:
can anyone give me some clues?

Peter Comaish

GOD'S PROMISE

See a rainbow arch in a rainswept sky,
Seven colours glisten in the sun's rays,
Red and orange, like fire's flames leaping high,
Join with yellow, green like sun on a bay.
Blue, indigo, violet - royal shades,
Complete the bow the Master set above,
When plucking Noah from a watery grave,
He made this promise showing His great love.
Harvest, in its turn, would follow spring birth,
Seasons would eternally come and go,
Never again would floods devastate Earth,
This the Lord God's message of the rainbow.
When I see His coloured arc flash above,
I'm assured of His promise and true love!

Pat Heppel

TO MY DARLING WIFE, MAUREEN

When I am gone from this place,
faraway, into the shadowed land,
no more to look upon thy face,
or hold thee gently by the hand,
and see the truth there in thine eye,
of your love, steadfast and true,
that I defiled with constant lies,
was faithless, weak and selfish too.
I hurt you badly, gave you pain,
heartbreak, sadness, and despair.
O! That I could live my life again,
and all my past misdeeds repair.
But time will not return the years,
not for my longing, not for my tears.

Still in the playground as a child was I;
but time has taught me how to grow,
to understand the wherefore and the why,
and I'm more sorry than you'll ever know . . .
Now I grow old . . . grow old and grey,
let not my voice fade in your ears,
my love go from your heart.
Weep not for me, and shed no tears
when I am gone, and we're apart,
but think about the things I've said.
Remember me when I am dead,
Do not let me die.

Huw Parry

OLLIE

Once you were a baby son,
That's obvious to every one
Those chubby cheeks have disappeared
Beneath the stubble of your beard,
Your plumply-fingered, dimpled hands
Have now more than an octave spanned
And what about those porcine toes,
So neatly wrapped in puppy fat?
No recognition now of those,
In bony digits long and flat.
The teeth that kept us all awake,
Can now demolish T-bone steak
Your coy, but sometimes wicked smile,
Some other female will beguile . . .
What happened to that child sublime?
Swiftly, swiftly, passes time
Long gone those shallow sighs of sleep,
When underneath the blankets deep
Your infant body softly breathed
Whilst all around the whole world seethed
Waiting, waiting as only time can . . .
To see the child become the man.

Heather A Hayne

RECESSION DEPRESSION

I can't write poems anymore
Poverty does not inspire
Creativity takes a dive
As interest rates soar higher.

What rhymes with repossession?
Litigation is also quite tricky
Cash flow becomes the obsession
Faced with a wicket so sticky.

My income and expenditure
Might make amusing reading
But writing verse makes others terse
When hungry mouths need feeding.

The total in the pile marked 'due'
Looks like the national debt
The sum that is needed monthly
Is three times the figure I get.

Writing poetry doesn't pay
And will not ease my strife
It's time to throw away the pen
And reach instead for the knife!

Kate Kerrigan

SUMMER

As we emerge from winters gloom
Into the sunlight and flowers bloom
No more fog, snow, wind or rain
Rheumatism lifts, so no more pain

Flowers come to life, the trees too
Birds are singing, Wood Pigeons coo
Hedgehogs wake up to venture out
Tortoises also and slowly no doubt

People are active there is so much to do
Car washing, repair jobs to name a few
Washing blowing, drying in mild breeze
Tidy up the garden and plant new seeds

As the days become longer and bright
We look forward, it becomes so right
To leave spring behind, not so sad
Welcome summer at last, so glad.

S Eason

DEDICATION

Being a nurse isn't much fun,
Your chores never seem to be done,
At everybody's beck and call,
You never have any time at all.
Fetching, carrying, running about,
Having to drop everything, when you hear someone shout.

Taken for granted, sometimes feeling like dirt,
Nobody cares if your feelings are hut,
But when a patient gives you a smile,
Everything suddenly seems worthwhile.
So, though being a nurse isn't much fun,
You get satisfaction from a job well done.

Maureen Arnold

THE KEEPING

As long as my old friends abide, intellect and will,
First love, I shall remember how we shared a moment then,
A bright and clear, late in February moment, when
Sea cliffs in clouds of lavender blue were dressed,
Cool chiffon clouds that hovered and caressed
Our shoulders like fluffy soft angora intumesced,
And our world stood anxious, breathlessly impressed,
While swaying and unsteady, you tightly held my hand
As we trembled, in our whirling giddy burst of spring,
And watched below blue larruped waters splashing, wavering.
Oh, I remember then! Oh, I remember when, so grand.
In keeping now, I hold you still in intellect and will,
For love remains my choice, this choice, love's choice, my bliss
And memory just my hand that holds your sweet love from abyss.

Edgar Wyatt Stephens

GEORDIE LAND

Grey waters of Tyne,
where there's rarely sunshine,
but, the people know how to
drink and to dine,
where things turn out happy if
it turns out fine,
and they can go down Shields
amongst the old brine,
while lots of old hinnys fill
their washing line,
there are still boy scouts who
make your windows shine,
some of our bad language we
could just refine,
still shimmering frost makes
a picture divine,
in this place we call Primrose
this birthplace of mine.

Jean Paisley

A VISION

Do you see her sitting on the rocks
That lady there with her little corgi dog?
A smile lights up her gentle face
As she watches the children on their surfboards race.

Listen! Now she calls my name
Can you hear her voice again and again?
'Oh Anne come in - the weather is changing
You'll get so cold if it starts raining.'

From the sea to the sand I quickly race
But she is not sitting in her place.
My clothes lie alone up on the rocks -
Blue jeans, white trainers and a pair of socks.

Surely it wasn't a trick of the light
I'm certain Mother was there with her smile so bright,
Maybe I'm wrong and it was just fantasy
But she did seem so real, so very real to me.

'Girls you shouldn't let the sun go down
On bitter words or angry frowns.
Patch up your quarrels before you go to bed.'
I hear the words of wisdom she often said.

I was not left rings to grace my hand
Mansions, riches or vast acres of land;
But something far more precious was left to me
A treasure chest brimming with golden memories.

Anne Haynes

A RAGING STORM

What is this sound, this noise of clanging?
Like Thor's heavy hammer or anvil banging,
'Tis thunder raging 'cross the sky.
With Apollo riding horses high.

Lighting tears a mighty rent
In blackened sheets of blankets, sent
To cover all the sky of blue
And brush away the sea of hue.

Torrential rain pours from above,
To drown the fields in lakes of love.
Swelling the rivers into mighty spears
That thunder down to ocean's meres.

It sweeps away the wasps in nests
That hide in banks of rivers - pests.
Boats, once moored along its banks
Go crashing to the sea as planks.

Mighty ships with keels of steel
That force their way through seas, and feel
Their way along once gentle rivers
Shy away from angry slivers.

People in houses near its edge,
Wake to find they are on a ledge.
Trees that grew by water's side
Are swept away with the angry tide.

Time will cure this world of rage
For only time can turn the page
Of life, and once again return
To the land of lands of which we yearn.

William Knapton

PRIME RHYME

I write my verses in rhyme all the time -
Much more expressive, I find than straight prose -
From the ridiculous to the sublime.

My mind draws a blank to verse without rhyme -
But where there's no rhyme - there's blank verse - I 'spose -
I write my verses in rhyme all the time.

From 'Poetry Now' young future bards climb
And poetic fame with sentiment pours -
From the ridiculous to the sublime.

Bards of renown with much pleasure I'll mime -
Poetic license my memory stores,
I write my verses in rhyme all the time.

When I'm past the age, oft times classed as prime -
In my true verse style - swan song I'll compose -
From the ridiculous to the sublime.

Spring clean-up now due and I'm faced with grime,
Cobwebs I'll brush from mind, ceiling and floors -
I write my verses in rhyme all the time -
From the ridiculous to the sublime.

Marian Curtis-Jones